Laying it out in a sketch (schetsmatig opzetten) *is the first foundation of drawing and is of such importance that you often achieve more through it than you can with great labor afterwards.*

If you search out the unique shapes of nature strikingly with the initial sketch, even the most elaborate works cannot compete with it.

—Sentiment attributed to Rembrandt van Rijn

For Love of Drawing

the drawing teachings of
Andrew T. McMillan
as recalled supplemented and presented

by **Tom Staley**

tomstaleystudio.com

Table of Contents

Lesson 1

Trust Your Eye

I teach beginnings, for years now, but terribly important.

What's the simplest thing that ties it all together? If you had one stroke to make the whole drawing . . .

Draw with your whole body, not just your wrist. That's why you're standing.

To the floor. There's got to be some kind of vertical in there.

You're trying to make them into arms and legs too soon. Don't draw the things, draw the patterns, draw the movements. You're following the *words*: Leg, arm, head, rather than your eye.

You want to put something in the drawing that makes it feel right from the beginning.

It might help you to imagine a string from here to there. Stretch the direction, let it go.

Now that gets us a start—a schema to work around.

Group them, group them. You've already got some details there that are going to prevent you from seeing it: It's too complicated, so you've got to find a way to simplify it. Group them.

See the things that are together, together: Feel them, place them, together. Sing:

All together now!

Work that whole curve. What an opportunity!
See if you can feel how full it is in here.
Don't get caught up in your detail here.
Squeeze that . . . give a little more there . . . pull that hand over . . .
Does that drop that much?
Watch your thicknesses.
Is that full enough yet to work against this?

To model: Open form please . . . Good. Thank you.

Go after that arch, get the feeling of it.

The idea that will help you is, I think, when you get a strong movement, just *follow through.* Like any other sport.

What's over what is a very useful thing. What's level with what is also a very useful thing.

Straights are easier than curves. Whenever you can find a straight, use it, because curves have a way of turning into mashed potatoes on you.

You've got to draw in such a way that you can criticize what you've done, otherwise you can't go on. You are writing information so as not to get in your own way.

Watch shift of lengths. You start with preconceptions of your sizes so you make the *same* size arms and the *same* size legs on the figure: You homogenize lengths. Give your eye priority in these judgements.

Right. It doesn't go there. It's trying to tell you something. What does it tell you about the shapes is your question now, not 'how can I fudge it.' *Don't put up with it.* If you see that kind of mistake you must do something about it right away.

Your placement is good, it's your sizes. They're a little timid.

Yes. Accentuate that movement. As you work, you begin to lose that gestural quality. You want to force it back to where it speaks. When you've been working on sizes and angles, it's difficult to make a stroke and that's that.

You're filling in there without being ready. Work the big design, it's easier.

You want the security of one thing in your drawing being exactly the same as the model, but I'm offering you a different kind of security: Your security, and the strength of your drawing, should come from the discovery and use of an overall big pattern, and not from details being exact.

It's much simpler to take that thing as a kind of rectangle rather than a leg, and you capture its essential quality.

Don't draw a head, draw a shape.

One of the hard things about drawing is that you have to trust your eye.

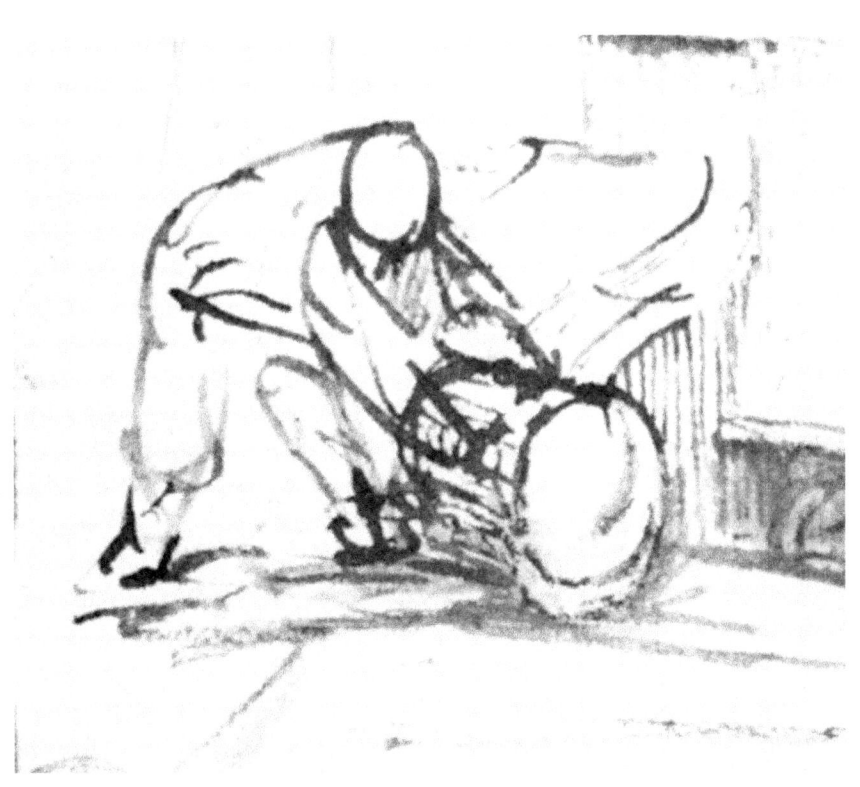

Lesson 2

Don't Think So Much

A post here. Get the whole thing. Get where the changes occur. Get the sizes. It's an abstraction.

Play a little bit before you get committed. Sometimes, if you grasp at it, it dissolves, where if you play with it . . .

You're leaving out one third of the sentence. You want to write the *whole* sentence first, and then re-write it: Don't leave things out now.

Don't divide it too much too soon. Group the whole business.

All these lines are forces that push you around the drawing. You want to find where these lines would take you if you extend them. What does this one strike . . .

You're looking for motives. Get the motive here: bolt of lightning.

Start your scale even earlier. Use the figure, or a part of the figure, as a scale-making device.

See, that space will help you all the way across the whole thing—space groups it.

Don't think so much. Why stop there? Carry it on down.

Take that block of space and compare it to that one. It's very useful to see what those sizes do for one another.

Go back a different route. Try and sense this size. If you don't go all the way, you won't begin to feel its size.

Your several large shapes have got to be definite enough so you can criticize them, clear enough to read them. These are too garbled. Clean it up, clean it up.

Be careful about tracing those edges. Squint. Laying down total areas is going to help you as much as the silhouette. If you just trace, copy, an outline, you lose the sense of how things join together.

You're picking at it too soon. Roll it together more. You're losing the motive. Make the details more subservient to the motive.

Stay at this stage longer. Whatever you put in you want to be clear so that it can serve in the design.

Learn how to move these shapes around. Learn to push the shapes in your drawing around, as an exercise in itself.

Build the block he's in to emphasize the *sides*. You should feature your side more continuously, as you would if you had a box. See, this whole side goes together.

Don't be afraid to cross the torso just because you want to find the *next thing* on the surface. Let your hand leap as freely around in the drawing as your eye does.

The drawing shows you as well. There's a conversation between the paper and your eye.

Use that plane there, that will help you. This thrust, how far. Make a judgment. This curve touches it here, if you want to give it a goal.

Squeeze here. Shift this. Enlarge this. Tie this in . . . You've got to struggle!

Student: You say the same things over and over.
McMillan: I know, and the funny thing is, it means something different each time.

Even more design.

Good, I still see it, the motive: bolt of lightning. Guard it.

If you sense it's a powerful movement, keep at it.

Let it go. Let yourself go.

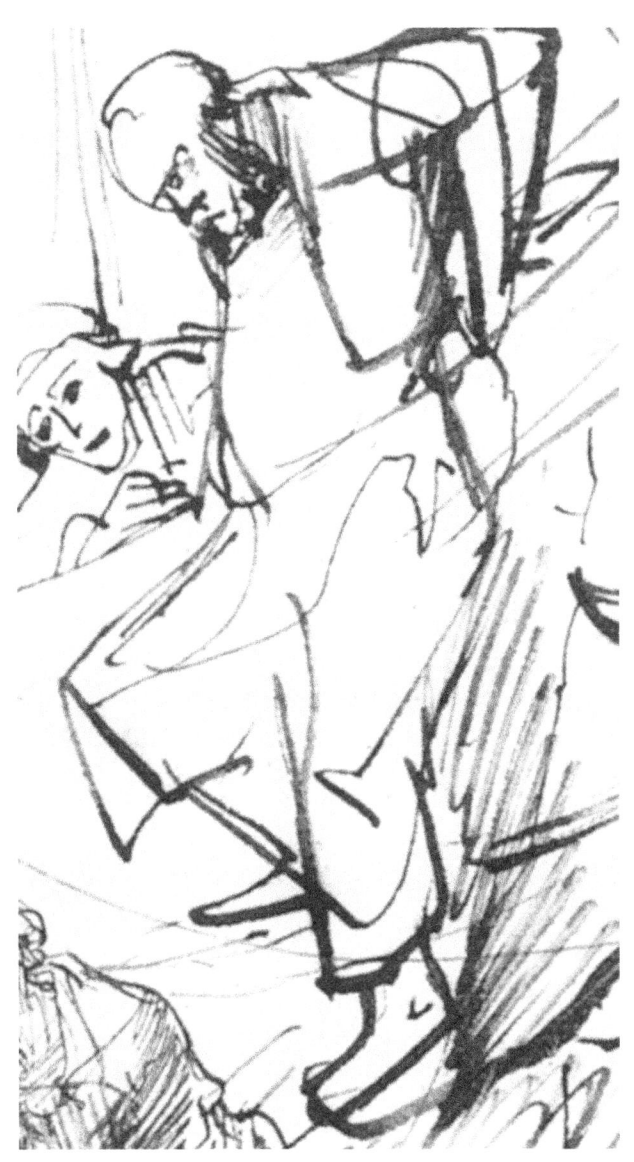

Rembrandt van Rijn

Lesson 3

A Kind of Still Energy

The trouble is, of course, that you see too much, so you have to kind of hold back—an appropriate reserve.

Watch two big things against each other.

These two directions meet here—diagonals. See, it's an energy, a kind of still energy, that you're building your design on.

Take more chances. You don't know what's down the slope, but slide right into it and find out. Go after it, go after it!

Establish something definite here so you can start judging. I'm having trouble reading across that way.

Get out of that section. Be a little more scatterbrained and come back at it differently.

Block this together. Lift this. Slide that down. What happens down here is not so intricate, but you need to have it set up to do what's above. You're really comparing above and below, and these sizes are going to help you. (I know, you don't want to have any analytical stuff at all, you just want to *draw*).

You're feeling around for something that's going to catch the *character*.

Yes. Burn that structure into your consciousness. Then, if you do something to disturb it later in the drawing, you'll know it's wrong. Learn to persevere with something strong.

Oh, you got a whole foot drawn. Hey, get your design to work first.

Get over the problem of having to caress each detail as you go along.

The solution to your problem: See both edges, not just one, and see how they work together.

Keep moving your eye. Follow the darks down. Bind it here. Close it up in here—tighten it down as a mass that holds together.

It's how you move your eye. Do it without thinking, because if you think, you'll stop. Trust your eye instead of just putting down what your mind conceives.

All the way around. This you've separated too much so it's fallen out of your design. Swing it all together and let the rhythm catch you.

Don't isolate your shadows. That tone has an attraction for itself. It's got to join together. Don't let it get too spotty.

Watch how the shadows play across the whole form: They're not so much local area things as you think. They go places.

Student: I do feel free with shading.
McMillan: Good . . . Feel the same freedom with boxes and spheres, with the structure, that you feel with tone.

What happens eventually is that your mind goes over these different ways of thinking about it with equal handiness as you need them, instead of just the last thing said to you.

It's a matrix of tone and a matrix of mass. If you can get what the mass does, you have more freedom to move around.

Get your drawing so you can read it.

Make it even more of a landscape.

How does the head work, how wide is it, relate it to the rest of the figure.

Get inside, come inside.

Don't go back the same way a second time.

You're tracing, following the edge. Don't trace, but react to directions and lengths, so you see a whole shape.

Student: So we're drawing shapes?
McMillan: Yes. Also, directions. Angles. Planes. Relationships.

Planes on the back. Got to make them or it won't be 3-dimensional. It'll be moiré paper design.

Step back, step back. Now we can see. Fix the head. Clean all this stuff up in here so you can accurately see what's going on. You have to get those ridges on the back where the form turns. Until you've got a corner, you're not going to get the light to operate on there . . . Now. Now you can get the tones to work on the back.

You pushed the edge extra hard at the last minute, didn't you. Even here. It stiffened it up a bit. Hmm. Try this: A lit edge, just dotted in--breathing.

Shadows give you the interior motives, to be used *with* edges before the edges harden, fossilize up. Use tone before the drawing gets so well made it's just coloring. Make tone a functional part of your drawing.

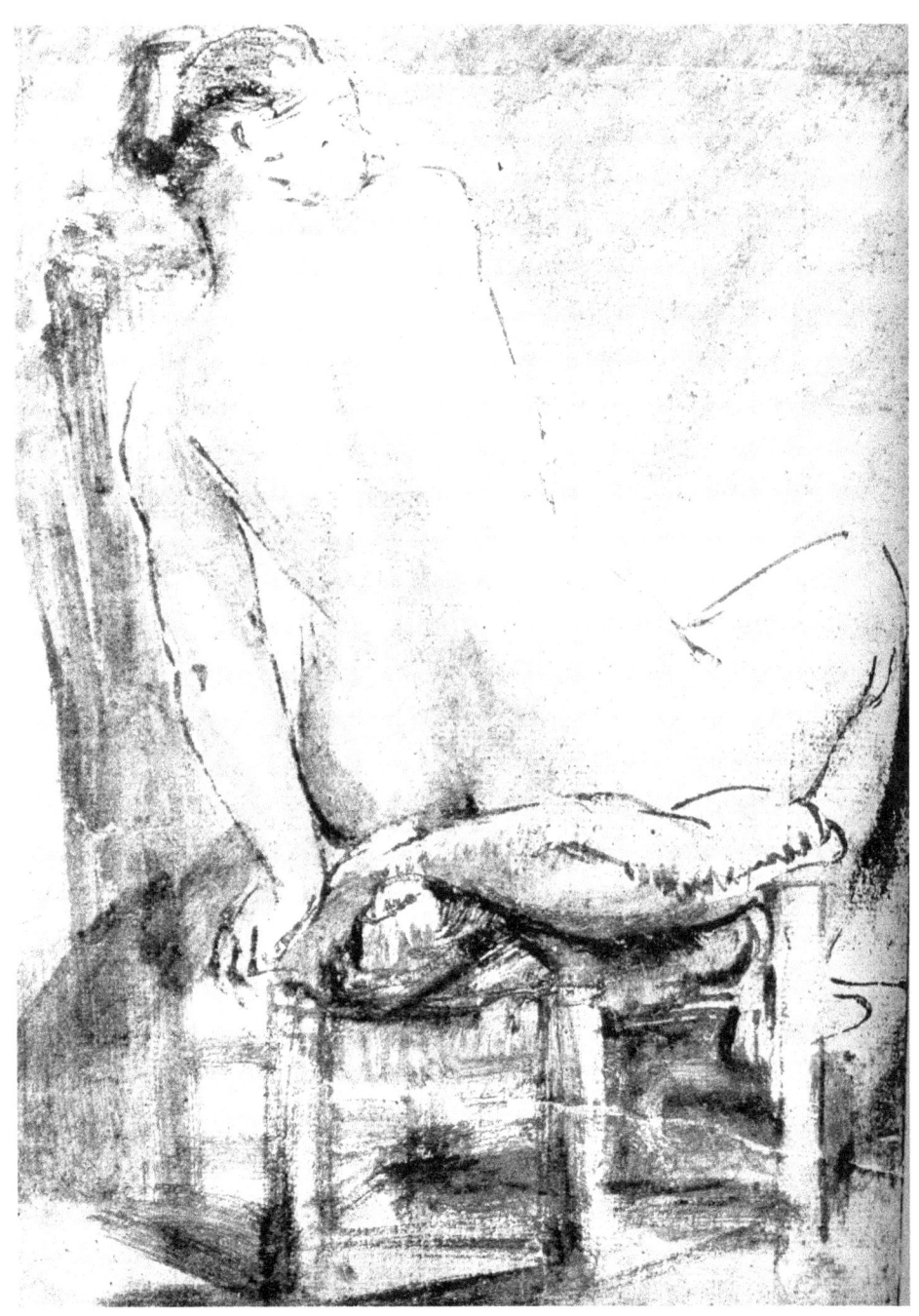

Rembrandt van Rijn

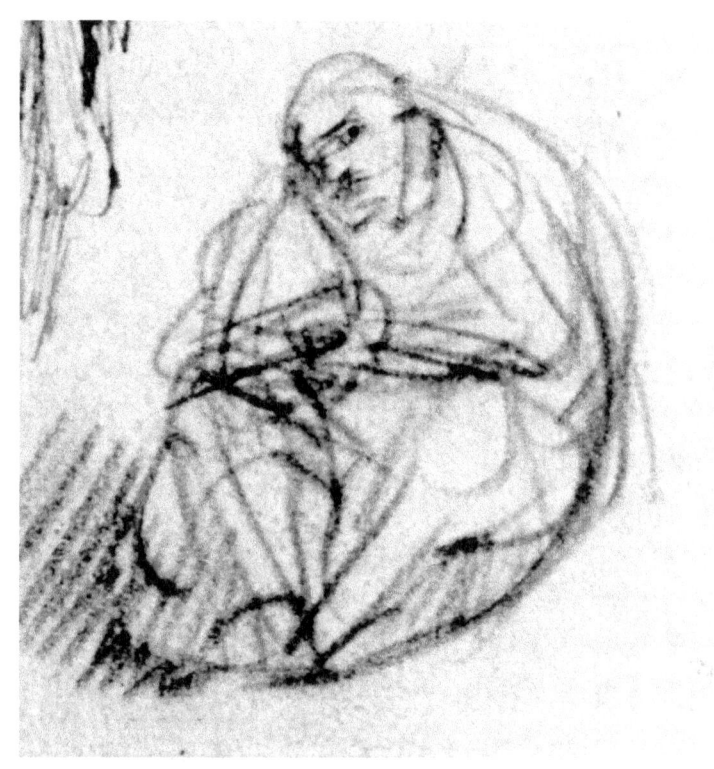

Rembrandt van Rijn

Lesson 4

Pattern Moves Your Eye

What's the shape of a block of wood you'd be looking for if you were carving him?

The longest simple thing that unites the whole.

Start anywhere, but move all around the thing. It's got this rhythm to it, if you deal with it as an abstraction. If you try to draw the things, you miss that rhythm.

See that backwards C? It's everywhere. It's the spine of your design. Spend a lot of time with it. What particular kind of C is it? The C is what demands your full attention and care, not any detail, not any thing. Is it tall? Is it tightly coiled? What's it's lean?

The tendency is to put something down as soon as you see it— but wait until you see it in relation to other things and to the whole.

The grouping is already getting too complicated. If you make it too complicated it will begin to get out of control. What you want to do is *not* complicate the issue, what you want to do is keep it simple. And very, very accurate in its simplicity.

If you have a problem, you tend to focus. But it's better to squint to see relations.

Let the natural design drive you around the drawing, don't draw one thing in isolation, then another, then another . . .

Watch the head. You're centering it on the rib cage from a preconception. Sometimes it's there but sometimes it's not. Because the head is supposed to be in the center of the body, you are misled. The cure is looking.

Something too attractive, dynamic, you tend to see in isolation.

One thing you've got to be able to do is change your mind. You make an estimate and if the estimate proves wrong, you have to be able to change it.

The spaces are going to help you a lot in this. This space: You haven't got its *vastness* yet.

Stay with how much and where. You have to be secure enough with the blocking to let other stuff flow out of it.

You're picking the wrong things. After half an hour, a page full of wrong things.

Good drawing, but no *motive*. Like a perfectly executed piano piece—but without feeling.

The motions you make are sort of like them—but you're not letting them go places.

To model: New one . . . Thanks.

Begin with the pattern.

There's an X. What *kind* of an X is your question.

Get the big angle, take it right off the model. Be precise in this.

You have to *make* him lean, or he won't lean.

In the beginning, not so much interested in separations of
shapes as how they connect.

If you draw the things, you miss the rhythm.
Work the spaces too—you're only working the silhouette.
There, there, there . . . skip that . . . a Morse code of shade.
After you make this, look at it. That's why you made it.

Pattern moves your eye. You're not really believing in them. If
you believe in them, they'll exist at the end of the drawing.

Follow through with your directions. The drawing is spreading
apart, and you must tighten it up, so push your directions. I
mean, extend your directions, *then* you can pull your parts
together.

These echo the clavicle, as though you dropped a pebble in a
pond. See, 1, 2, 3 . . .

Feel it as a mound. That lets you disengage it from anatomy and
see it.

What you don't want to do is do the same thing over and over
again. You need something to refresh your eye.

Lay something down and find some movement that'll take you
out of that area.

You've got to make it say 'head,' and when you do, it'll be much more of a figure.

Good. You're trying to lay it down all at once more than you have for some time. Check those horizontal bands.

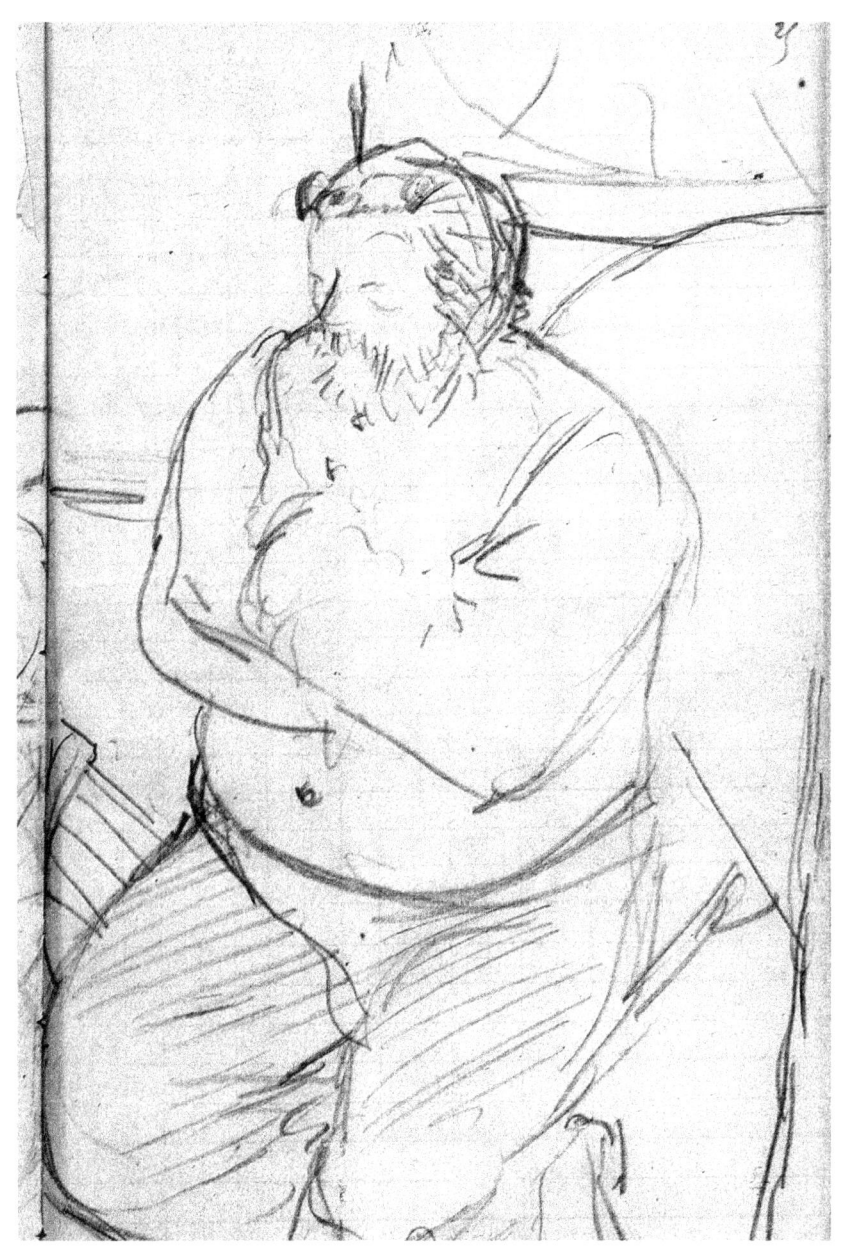

Edgar Degas

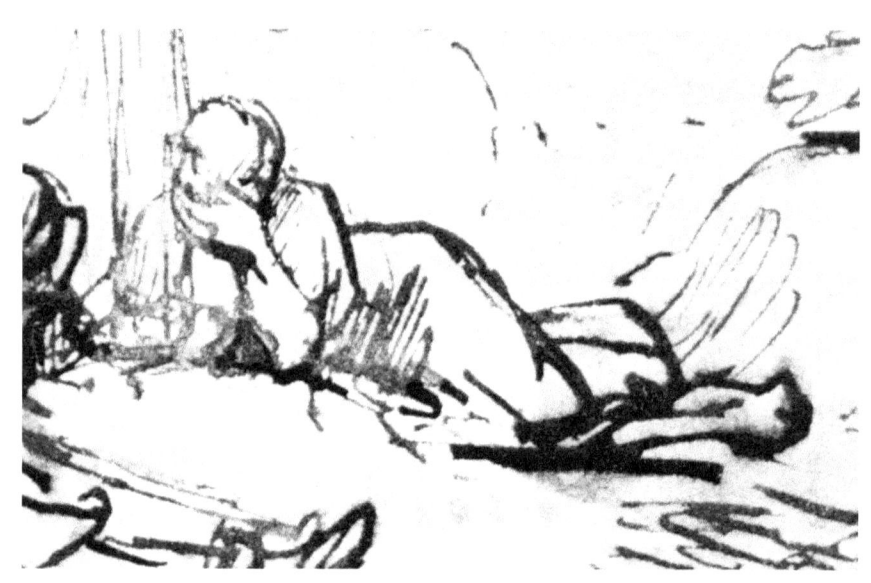

Rembrandt van Rijn

Lesson 5

You've got to Decide and Decide and Decide

What kind of a shape. If we covered him with a sheet, what would he look like?

Don't get caught up in the little stuff. You're impressed by the enormous variety in there: Make the *group*, then fit the pieces in.

Don't get wedded to that. You're trying to do it too soon, before you find out where it is, its location.

You've overdrawn a part, you've decided too much what goes in there. No leeway left. Let the drawing grow organically. You're thinking: This . . . is . . . the . . . thigh . . . . Look for the connections more. Your eyes think like your hands, exploring, groping, caressing broadly.

You need something to hold your description together.

I'm worried about it down there. You're letting go of it, the feet.

What *kind* of a triangle, what kind of a triangle, what kind of a triangle.

That's a mistake. Don't put up with it, and you'll learn. If you can't move it or change it any more, consider ripping your paper up and starting over. I can't tell you anything easier to do.

Watch the generalization of that against that direction.

Work with the shapes more. You're not making them definite enough.

Don't accept what you've drawn just because you put it there. The problem is, you want to put it down and have done with it. But you've got to decide, and decide, and decide.

Get that pattern going for yourself, be loose enough to fit those shapes together. If you're overly careful, you lose it.

Find out where it goes. Drive it through more.

Something very simple: How wide for how tall.

Step back, step away from your drawing. Now, look at it. You have to let it talk to you. You talk to it by drawing. But it is a two-way conversation.

You're making it too complicated. Start brutally simple, then you can use your skill, and keep the brutally simple pattern through the drawing.

Group against group.

If you change and work with shadow pattern, it might freshen your eye.

He's more languid than that, his posture.

Why don't you go to the end of this thing—the sweep of this arm into the other.

You're staring at it. Watch out: Section by section. Find what will fit into your design, build from the truth of your design.

Draw the head *with* something else, then it will go on.

He's more monumental than that, the length of his side.

Keep building your drawing as though you were just starting it and you'll find more things to do.

See, you've got to *try* for those connections, they don't just happen. Otherwise your drawing will look like it's coming apart at the seams.

Work the space inbetween.

Tom, you're beginning to open up some. Something's happening with you and line that allows you to move them. You're able to grow with your drawing.

Don't be afraid to make a mess.

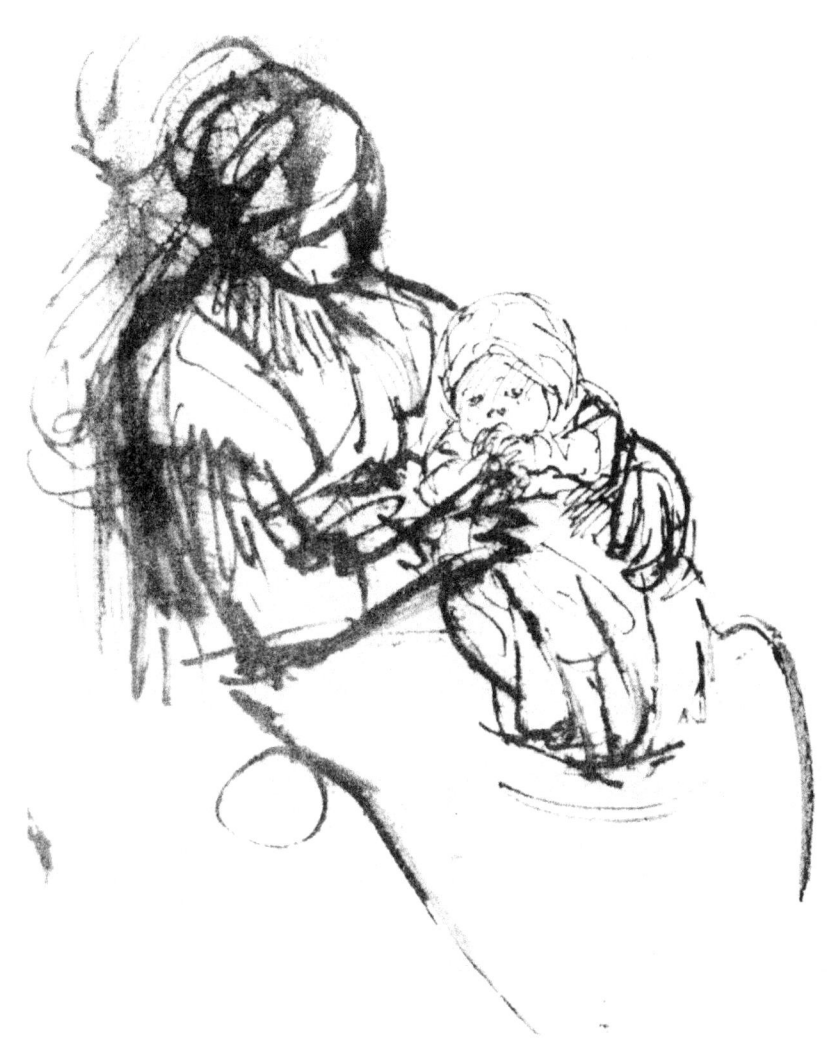

Lesson 6

A Feeling of Freedom in the Drawing Action

Make some shapes. If you have trouble getting around it, just some mass.

One of the things you have to do is trust that you will find something.

Make her stand.

Draw the groupings.

Don't stop, don't stop, don't stop.

Okay, step out.

You want to see that big shape and let it control the design. You'll never see it as clearly as now, at the start of the drawing.

Looks like it might be a triangle, what do you think.

Put the string on the bow to check the width: How wide for how tall.

How do you know it's there? Make it stretch and tie it onto this business. Begin to locate it.

When you see a movement, follow it, don't resist it.

Get enough there so you can test it. Pull it together—find a way to get from there to there, so it will read. Just a little pressure here—bring it up—watch it from there—what level is this—what level is that.

Watch out that you're not just tracing edges. If you draw the silhouette in, you don't have that chance for reprieve.

Make the spaces. Holes are very good on this one. Get your holes set up.

Don't worry about the wiggles too much, just worry about those two great big bars hitting each other.

You're doing well, you're drawing in terms of totals: Total areas, two or three big total areas—in terms of light and shade here.

Don't break that up too soon. There'll be some small movements in there, but they can wait . . .

As you're drawing that try to feel it to the patella.

Line up the heel with the light change on the arm.

To Model: Change the shape please.

New pose, back to beginnings, loosen up.

You cut the head off because it's difficult, but if you don't get the whole length of that post, the abstraction, right from the beginning, then it's not nearly as dynamic a composition.

You're trying to do too many things before you get 2 or 3 big things. If you divide it too much you won't get the simplicity of the shape.

The distances between the extremities are very important. Tie them together, invent a measure and a shape to tie them together.

This drives harder, with tremendous energy.

That's where you want to spend your time--really *caress* that thing that you're doing.

A lot of this drawing will be this enormous space.

Sometimes you have to relax your focus and let it go to see how a shape fits with the rest of the drawing. Hard to do.

Stand back and look at it: Very often, when you make a size error it depletes the energy of the drawing.

I'm trying to make the design stronger to tell me about that shape. I want to relate the shape to the design, but loosely enough so I can still work with the shape's size.

The beginning of this drawing for you was a trapezoid. Stay with it, then the drawing won't get away from you. You're getting grasped by a single part, and it's not located. Once you get done being seduced by that part, you won't know where to go from there.

You need a track to run on, an abstraction that encompasses the whole drawing, so that you can move from place to place in it with freedom, without the fear of getting lost. It's going to cost you something to search out those broad design elements, but your reward will be a feeling of freedom in the drawing action. You just can't underestimate what that feeling of freedom, of ease, will give to your drawing.

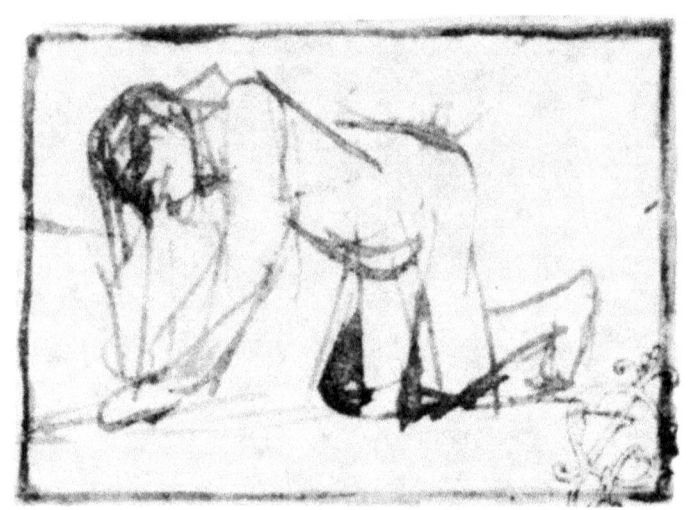

Rembrandt van Rijn

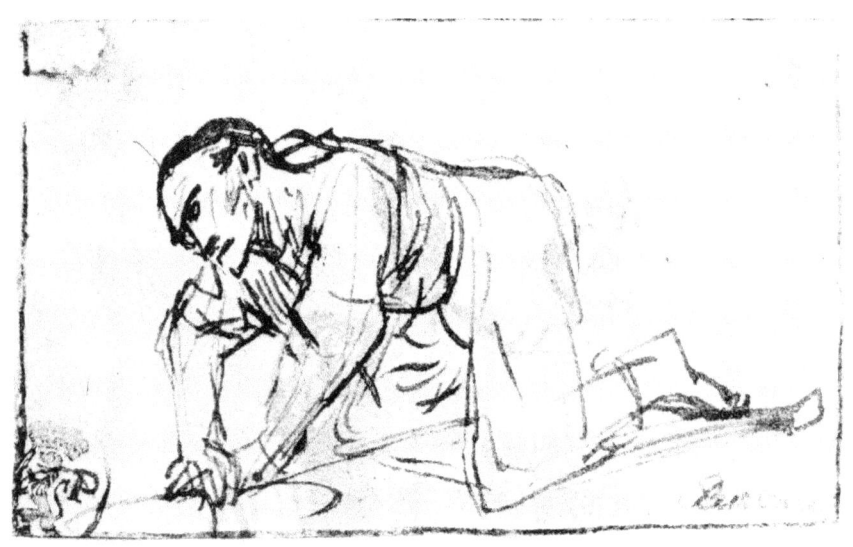

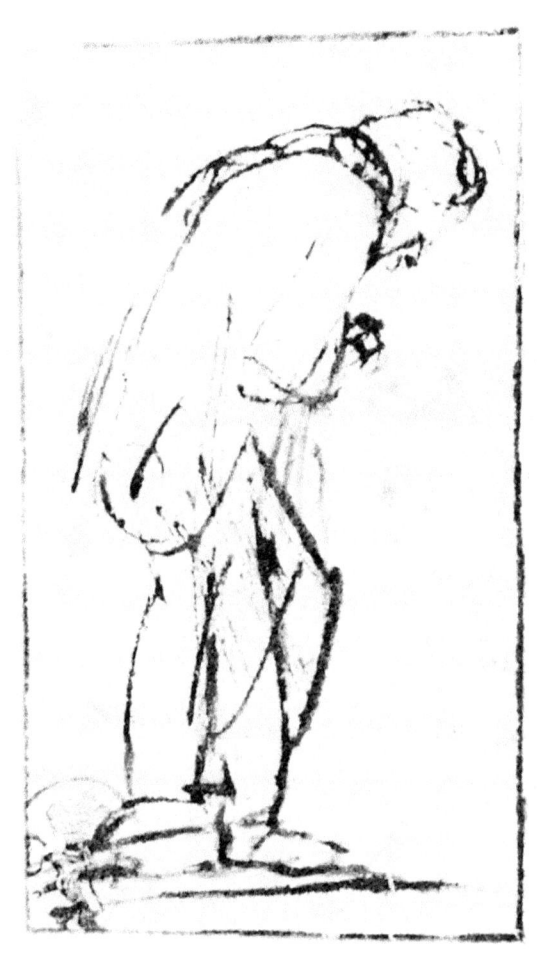

Rembrandt van Rijn

Lesson 7

A Non-Stop Response

Go.
   Don't think, draw.
   Put them there, you'll know what to do.
   Find the longest thing you can, from one end to the other.
   Stretch them through, you'll find more information.
   See this force, it's like a comet or something: Shwww . . .
   Get all this.
   Go ahead. Find the floor. What happens here.
   It's a non-stop response!

Make a shape.
   What kind of a shape.
   Make a shape out of it. *Just draw that shape.*
   Then, let it divide into large units.
   All the way across, from here to here.
   Lift the head.
   Pull the head right out of the torso.
   Keep moving on it. Get the bigger shapes.
   This works off of that.
   One, two . . . how they fit together.
   Feeling of this triangle penetrating that space.

Step back.
  Your angle here is not okay. She's steeper.
  Watch this against that.
  Longer here. You're probably okay with your width.
  Level with what.
  Look from the back of the head to the floor.
  See the box. Almost a square.

You're looking at this part without relation to anything else, one
    thing then the next one, sequential, and it's going to come
    together I don't know when.

Hmm. Got the feeling, but located wrong. Got to work on the
    broad design.

You can build a drawing on just these rhythms: Parallels.

You can't afford to look at that by itself and dissect it from its
    environment. In conjunction with the arm it makes a shape.
    If you look at it by itself, you don't see that.

Make a triangle and she'll fit in. Let's round out the back more.
    Pull the shoulder out more. The head is one of the things
    that is most difficult. Take the plane of the face and drive it
    all the way to the hand.

Make the shapes, not the 'leg' or 'hand' or 'head.' If you make
    the shapes, you can move around the page freely because
    you don't have an investment in it. You don't own a house.

Let this penetrate. Lift this. Very wide. Put the bottom on.
    Squeeze it together here. This flows right into that. Shorten

that. Straighten the arm here. Then, get this thing attached, if you possibly can . . .

Student 1: "Lift," "squeeze," "push," "kick," "drive," "stretch". . !
McMillan: It's an *activity*.
Student 2: "Non-stop response."

Play with these—just long enough to locate them. Don't get caught on the silhouette. The problem is, a silhouette isolates an area, you can't break into it and out of it.

Pull this out of the dark. Get this strong movement. Now link this up here, start that tone there. See what I'm doing? That value is going to hold it together.

Give yourself a clean space to work in here—very difficult to make size judgments with that jumble of lines in there.

You've got this so complicated you're allowing it extra space. It's really just an L, isn't it. You have everything but the pattern, the L shape. See, once you insist on its L-ness, you can gauge its size in relation to the rest.

You're hitting it on the outside, the silhouette. It's getting hollower and hollower. It's a tricky drawing. Why trace it?

Staley: I've been looking at Renoir's studies for The Bathers. His silhouettes work so well.
McMillan: Someone who has sought volumes his whole life can handle silhouettes. Shhh. Draw.

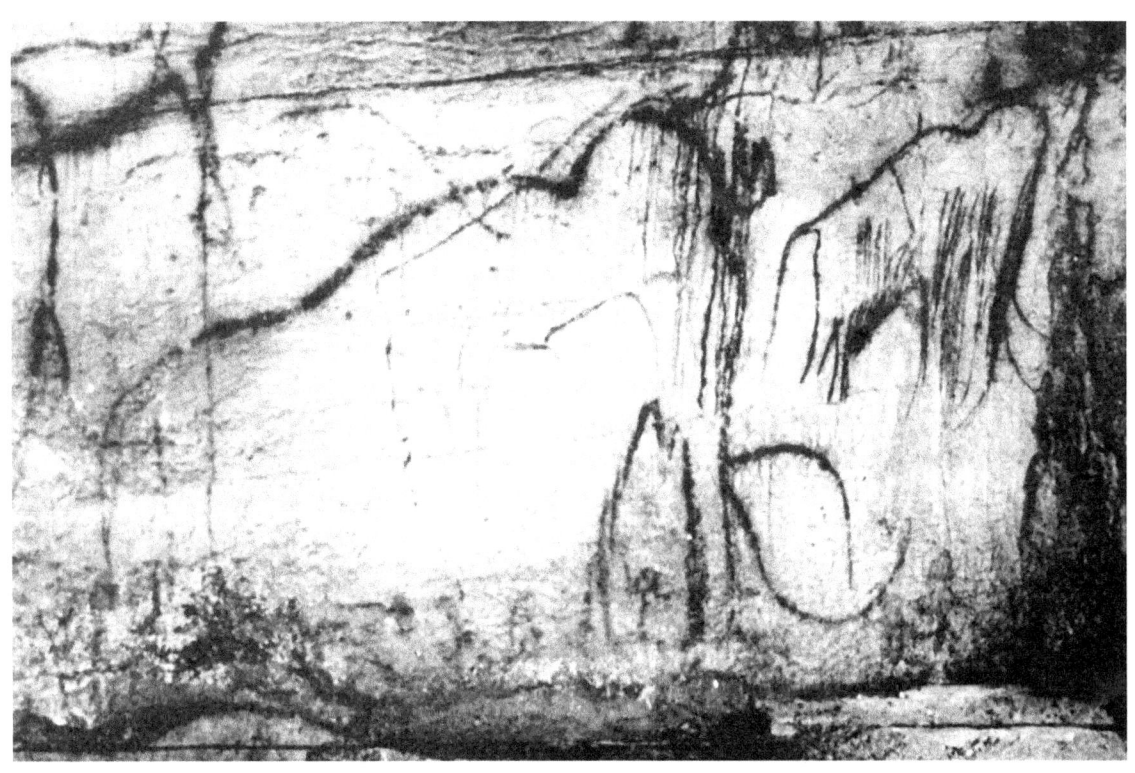

Paleolithic Artist, 18,000 B.P.

Lesson 8

It's Hard to Get it Simple

You can't draw them one by one. They won't go together.

Big shapes, big overall shapes. Got to see the whole thing.

Don't start with the smallest, start with the largest.

Drive this to the floor. This against it. Set this up very strong, very accurate.

Make some big move like that, then step back and see if you're screwing yourself up.

It'll work. You have to stay with it long enough. A triangle, then there's a big shape in there—it's all out of this triangle. A little height there. A little fuller here. Ah, that makes that shape better, doesn't it.

You can adjust it to work out of that structure. You're making a hanger for your drawing to attach to. It's more than a hanger though. A lot of the real feeling of the piece will come from it.

Yeah? With what up here? Use your vertical, locate your shoulder. Watch now: How much to the left of it and what shape. Get your stick out and push the vertical further—to the corner of the skull? Make the corner of the skull. With this, and this, you've got the whole shape of the head out of these directions.

McMillan: Like I said, you can't draw them one by one. They won't go together.

Student: How else can I draw them but one by one!

McMillan: See them together, draw each as part of something else--curve or direction or shape. Always something that relates them to the whole.

Got to lean it. These angles are stronger. You're feeling it, but not strongly enough. The tendency of course will be to make it completely upright.

The shape of the space between the legs is easier to see than the legs themselves.

What you have here is much too complicated for the organization you have so far.

As a group, what do they do as a group. It's not hard to get it complicated, it is hard to get it simple.

The whole shape—ah, missing the angle. Got a straight edge? Can't make the drawing unless you can make the angles. Take those steps back to see it. You don't need me here to see it.

You want to be very sure how those abstract sizes and shapes fit together or things will expand too much because there are a thousand wrinkles in there.

Don't draw the leg, draw the *direction* on the leg.

Don't just drop this, work on it, relate it. Make an analysis.

Don't try to make the little wavelets.

Don't get too complicated. Upside down styrofoam cup shape, right? Go with it.

Good design. Promote it.

Going to cut a little out. Now, I may have overdone it. Squeeze it a little bit over. You can squeeze those shapes. My system is, I go way over then I go way under, and strike a balance. Faster than inch by inch.

This is getting too large. A detail, but it's telling you something. You've got to keep checking those things using the design you've developed so far. Fix it now! Don't leave it. Bad for you, junk food. Get your machete out!

You're just going round and round the drawing. Kick it in, use it right up trying to make it right. Better to throw it away than teach yourself to make a bad drawing. Do away with this tentativeness, get in there with something strong and make it right.

You're really making your locations work. You've got a rhythm going in the drawing. I'm not objecting to making lumps, wavelets, *if* they're tied to those structural beams. Follow those major movements and keep that rhythm going.

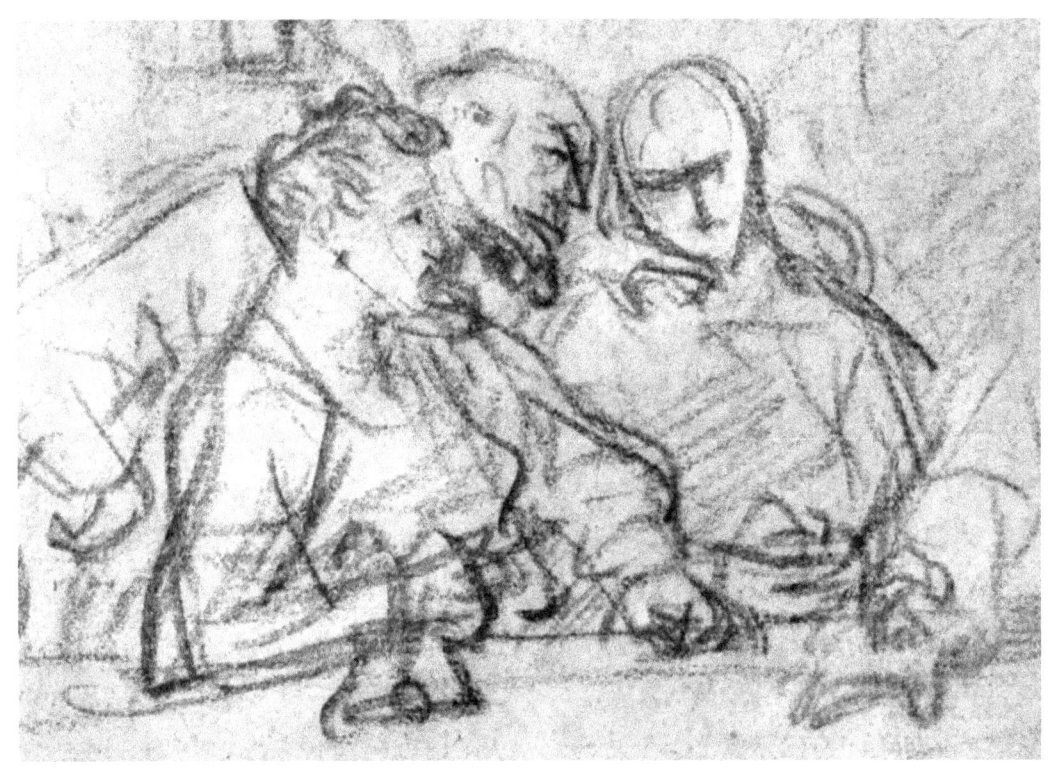

Rembrandt van Rijn   55

Lesson 9

Work the Shapes

To model: Give us a rolled up one.

Tough drawing to make, but sure is a beauty.

Feel that bend of the arm—step out, step out, and you'll see it immediately: A reclining J.

Start feeling this here. A lot of it takes place inside the body. Take your stick. You've blocked that. That's the design very strongly that way . . . You have the luxury of a good start.

That's how you get the feeling: When you work the shapes. See that? Wineglass shape. Isn't it wonderful?

The mouth is on a line inside the shoulder girdle—has to go way down. Got to stay with that awhile—it'll look awful. Don't look at the head separately: It's on this big directional, and one third of it is inside the body. Stay with it. The head is always a problem. This zygomatic is going to relate right on to the direction of the arm. See it?

This has to kick out, it's a big curve, all the way to the knuckles. When this edge hits the knuckles, we're way the hell out in space. And it doesn't fit on the page! . . . That's a killer . . . You should find that out in the first minute and adjust your scale.

Horizontal movement. A band. Useful. When you look at *things* you don't see that.

You're putting down stuff that has to occur 15 or 20 minutes from now, without having the pattern. Stand back. What's that curve. Don't want to see any bumps on it. Want to see this simple crescent thing.

It's very interesting, it's a nice parallelogram to work with. Take your stick and run it along the right side of it.

Drive those directions, then see how those shapes work out.

You're putting light and shade on because you see contrast, but the mass and direction of tone is what you want.

Squint, and you'll see how much bright light against how much shadow. Use those value groupings, let them criticize and reinforce your other pattern.

If you can tie your masses together and tie your values together to make a believable space, if you can do these two things-- you will be a good draftsman.

Everywhere the same pressure of the pencil. It's stifling.

Looking at drawings: Your feeling and body response dictate where you look. Here, too.

You're separating. You've got all these little pieces separate from the others. It's hard to see how they go together.

That's straight from your brain, not from your eye. I'm watching this dimension and that dimension, 'how tall is she for how wide.' It's real simple.

If a drawing doesn't work and you can no longer see to alter it, rip it up, start over. If instead you treat yourself to this terrible indulgence, you'll never know why it's constantly wrong, you'll be too busy covering it up all the time.

It's got to be moreso to get the shape.

We're in some danger here. This mass must be large enough to keep that mass small. See what I mean?

This D shape—be careful about regarding it as a separate entity. This boat shape: Both of these together give you the unity of the design. This tone crosses and simplifies it. That's good. Keeps it simple enough to see it together again. You were cutting it all up in 1/8 inch pieces. First, get it set, the design. It's crazy, but it works.

This stuff here that you haven't even got to yet has got to roll together with this. You're taking it so slowly that you're missing the unifying factor. That's what I'm teaching, how to move your eye to get that unifying factor to refer to in the rest of your drawing.

Hallway after class, two chairs

McMillan: All this resistance.

I see how few of them are learning from me.

They won't listen to my advice. It's like putting bread in a toaster and it pops right back up cold and untoasted.

Almost impossible to make them see ensemble. They don't do the blocking at all, just rendering. Bit, by bit, by bit.

Staley: The immediate rewards always go to rendering: 'Wow, what detail.'

Student approaches

Student: What is drawing?

McMillan: Drawing is an essential trained way of seeing. It allows you to see in an orderly way.

Drawing is a product of design, that is, design is paramount to perceive.

The space and the form are absolutely integrated, space and form are seen together.

Drawing is a training in making things go together.

Student: How do you learn to draw?

McMillan: You have to search out the instruction.

Take the reins. Only if you attempt things will you learn.

In the end, it's up to you.

It takes courage.

Learn it now.

Something very difficult about drawing is that you can't evaluate your progress in the same way you can in learning how to weld, from a manual. To know where you are is very confusing.

Staley: The words matter. Remember pertinent sayings you overhear spoken by the teacher to other students. Later, try your own drawing under the spell of one or another of those teachings. Explore their meaning in the drawing action.

McMillan: Maybe. I think the opposite, too. There's the physical aspect. You get engrossed, hammer and tongs, and you're in a different place, where there are no words.

Student: Thank you.

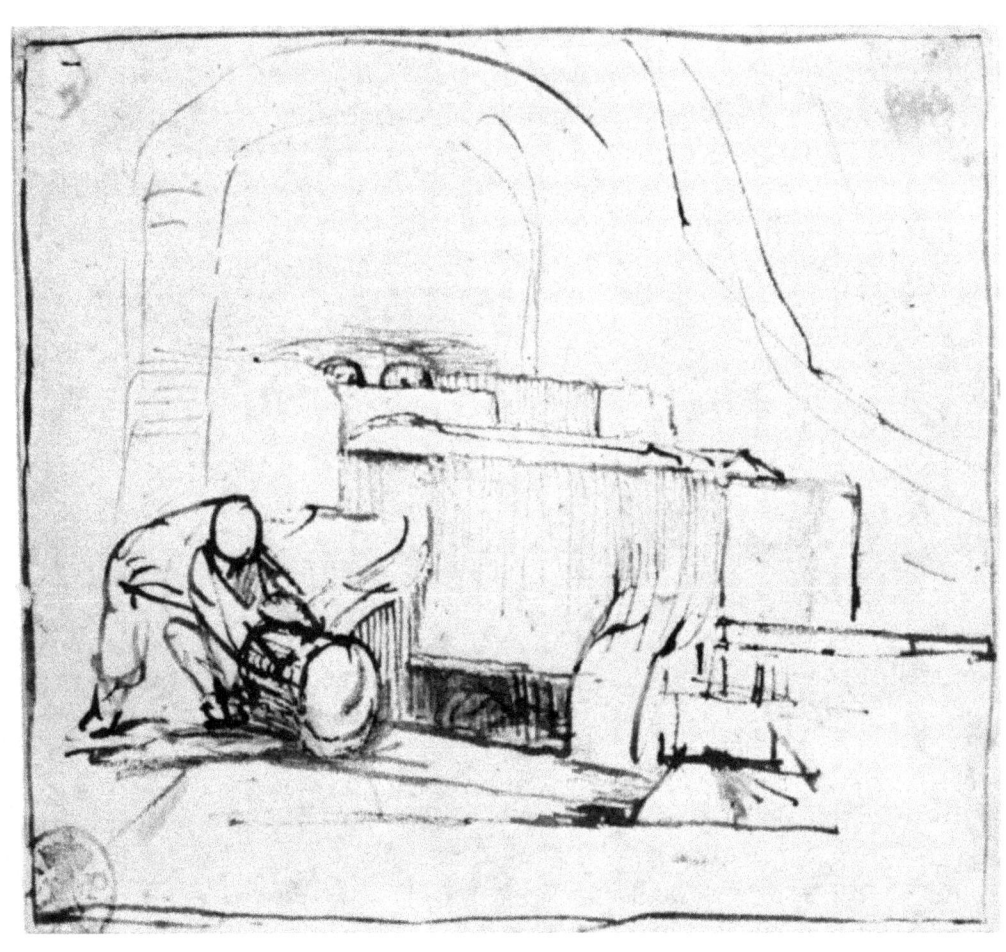

Rembrandt van Rijn 63

Lesson 10

Never Stop Pressing for Unity

Clay Sculpture Class:

McMillan: When I was a student at the Museum School, I saw a show of Rubens' drawings. What I saw was a vision of *the facility to draw*. That was what I wanted out of art school. I had to seek out a teacher outside of the school though, George Demetrios. He approached drawing from a sculptor's point of view: Ability to analyze in simplified shapes for a performance in sculpture, where you are assembling all these viewpoints. You learned to be very accurate with what you were doing with those shapes, so they made a unified 3-D object. A painter can fudge a bit— inexact angles, sizes—because he's using only one view. Sculpture trains you in complete plastic assembly.

Set yourself up: Work the armature. It's a rough adjustment that forces you to begin seeing.

Very simple pose: Standing man.

Your view clicks, a strong pattern.

The whole shape, the whole shape. All the way to the top. Include the leg. Put it on now.

Make sure you walk. For standing figures, get away from your piece.

Your composition is the two blocks. Make the bottom block work with the top block. This whole block, not just this silhouette. You're missing how the block goes, and you're catching a little piece of the silhouette. Come back and look: Compare everything underneath there with everything above. When you begin to neglect the top, lower your stand.

Put it there, take it out, put it there, take it out: Sculpture is like that. Eventually you figure out the balance you want.

You have a dynamic that works. You've found your project.

McMillan rotates model a quarter turn on his stand. The students turn their stands a corresponding quarter turn.

New view to work.

Use the X pattern, right out of that side into that one. It locates the head. Widest here, second widest here.

Work silhouettes. Unlike drawing, in sculpture much of the work is done on silhouettes. That's where you take clay off or put it on because you can't see well, you can't make accurate depth judgments, building the clay in front of yourself, towards yourself. In making sculpture, depth often comes from the combining of views of the silhouette.

From your view: Bigger triangle. Head-toe-little finger. See your shape. Get a view that's big enough.

Be careful about working in little areas—you do it in drawing, too. It's not drawing, and it's not sculpture.

Interesting: Stack stack stack, a rhythm of parallel elements. You look for something like this! You want to grasp an overall gestural rhythm like that, then if you do something later that perpetrates a wrong against that rhythm, you'll feel it. It's your design and it gives you a handrail all the way through the process.

Cut there. Pat it there. Taller, taller. Much, much narrower in here for that thickness.

What sits on top of there. And this. Draw and cut. Don't worry in this view about what you've got to do in the next view.

You're scooping it too much—you're not seeing the external oblique, so you're overdoing this invasion into the body.

McMillan rotates the model a second quarter turn.

Again: Clay, it's difficult to put it on or take it off in front of you. Mainly, work the silhouette.

Look at the view you've got now: Elliptical shape in plane across his body, like that. Very fascinating. I think you'll feel it.

You're not seeing this: Spear point. It isn't happening in your piece.

You'll save yourself so much time if you take those three steps back. Rhythm of work, and three steps back.

The head's got to go forward to continue this bar.

No, you're concave in the back. Watch what happens with the stick. *Holds stick parallel to back of model.* Watch that space. A straight tells me how to do the curve.

Lift this. Higher. Chip this extra flesh out.

The rib cage is not a barrel. It is approximately a barrel, for you for now from this view. Wait for your next view, you'll see.

Not enough of a curve. You have 15 details. Just make the curve. Not enough left—to right—to straight. Do you feel it? You're not going to feel it till you see it together.

Okay, you're building *parts*. Build whole sweeps, build the big organizational fact. I'm seeing something of a continuous swing here. You need to get your distance. This is still about seeing.

Watch out for the concave here. I'm very worried about that.

Keep stretching that big elliptical ring, then bend it forward.

There is no concave in the back. You're not just going to add a little piece there and fix it. It's masses moving in space. Dynamic. Not contour drawing on clay, but masses relating.

Only one eighth inch of concave.

McMillan turns model third quarter turn.

Don't stare at it, reduce it. Often you reduce it too much, but you're back in the ball game. Do not accept a diminishment of your goals by allowing that kind of error to continue.

Push the clay. Don't add stuff now. Pound it in there.

You put one thing or other right, then it tells you: 'Those planes are intersecting at a different angle from what you have.' It doesn't tell you what to do there. It does say: 'Fix it, fix it, fix it.'

McMillan turns model fourth quarter turn.

A standing figure is opposed to gravity. The Greek Kouros is a symbol of that culture, and of its vitality.

Student: Clay is easier than drawing, to me.
McMillan: Then treat your drawing as clay sculpture.

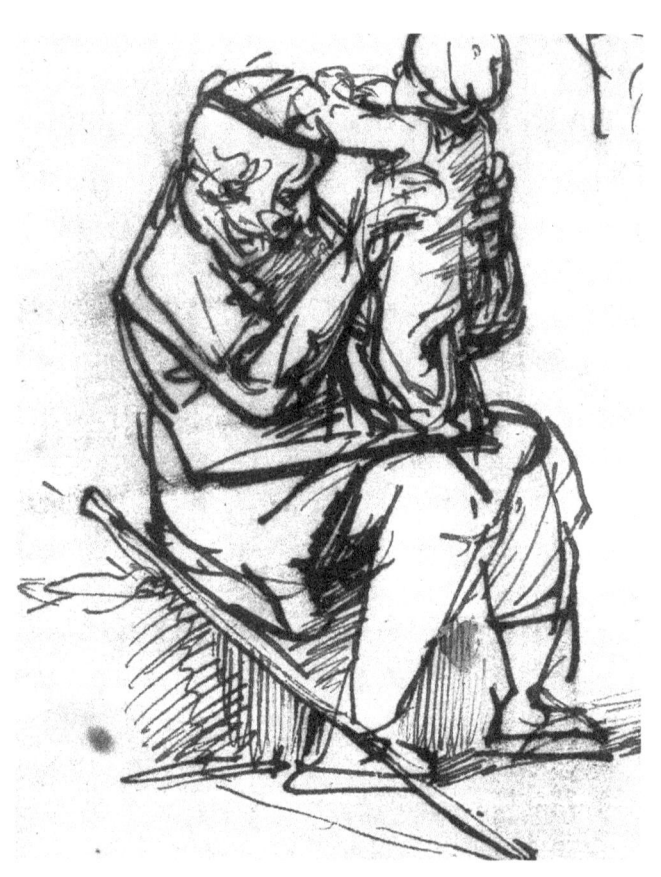

Rembrandt van Rijn

Lesson 11

Set the Whole Sheet in Motion

I'm trying to get a sensibility of what the total image is, from the beginning, so I won't get lost. My teacher used to call that total image 'the ensemble.'

I'm asking you to respond to what the patterns tell you to do, not to your thinking. It becomes a very exciting learning process, not just putting down ideas from your head.

See two or three shapes, then use some other pattern to check what you have.

The rib cage yeah, and on top of the rib cage is the scapula, yeah. Now what I want to see is—around and around—tone in here to keep that spherical shape going. Don't get suckered in by these concaves. The whole thing must feel very convex.

Drive this through so it doesn't just happen at the top, but at the bottom, too. Then it's organized so the forms are held together. All of a sudden, we're getting space in the drawing, too.

You've made two different pictures on two different scales. You're seeing this and this, but not the connector.

See how this feeds into that? Closer with that. Cut it down there. See now: 1, 2. So, I'm using this big geometry to help relate it. (Are you stepping back when your draw? Sort of! You gotta!)

I'm going to make the geometry of the rib cage stronger. This plane and that plane. This corresponds to one side of a milk carton, this to the other side. We're keeping things from breaking apart.

I'm not first of all making a unity of value, but a unity of how this thing is connected. It's the priority of the issues, to you, that will cause you to draw more one way or the other. You might want to look at Heinrich Wölflin on this matter.

Not so jagged.
Don't stay in that isolated area, get out of it.
Bigger pieces.
The whole thing, the whole thing, you only have a piece of it.
What's the top of it. Make a composition of it.
Make the whole sheet work. Set the whole sheet in motion.

Don't leave the head off. In this case it's part of the arm. Anatomy books say it's not, but it's part of the arm this way, and it's part of the arm that way.

Don't get caught working just one section or, if you do, immediately connect it back to the larger entity.

When you make your groupings, don't make just one large one and divide it. Make several, and relate them.

You're working it like you're writing a letter, from top down. Instead, do the impossible: Do it all over, all at once. Might require some jumping. Extremities are to be related, your design should do that.

You are building it in local relations only. Instead, build relations that go across the whole image. A larger kind of relating.

You want to stretch them as far as you can, across the whole image.

Everything I'm teaching basically is construction drawing— you're an architect, right?

I'm feeling these sides. The important part is not the 'style,' the important part is to deal with them together. Don't aim deliberately at style—at this stage, at least. Just tell the truth.

See, I'm looking at them as shapes and then modifying them for perspective. If you see them as arms instead of shapes, you can't see them objectively, as you need to for this foreshortening.

Get this background thing so we can feel space behind the figure. Everything's meeting there: Floor-line, post, shadow.

This black. And you've got to move it. Need eraser. Watch these two sizes instead of thinking. How much light flash for how much dark flash. And get a pink pearl eraser for your charcoal.

The original movement I'm seeing to do this is a gestural sweep from the foot into the head. The other movement I get now is on that side. Use both.

Good. You've fixed how those two big groupings go together. Guard it, so that if you do something that disturbs it, you will question what you've done.

Squint to look at it.
See this, 30-caliber bullet shape.
I'm placing the highlight.
Head gets set against this tone.
Relate this to a larger motive.
Here, work with the concept: Plane meets plane in line.

Take this down in tone and make it work in the whole. Use your eraser and break the tone down enough so it sits back. And with the edge here: You've kind of traced it. You're working the edge over and over again so it's jumping off the page. Break the edge up and work inside more.

You see, you're not really making a drawing, but locating masses. Don't you dare draw that thigh yet. First and last, locate masses and accede to big movements.

Lesson 12

Details Don't Make Up a Drawing

1, 2 first, not: 1, 2, 3, 4, 5 . . . It has to hold together as a two
   first.

Push the planes, simplify.

I wouldn't look at that at this moment—look at the rectangle.

Watch the intervals—how long, how long, how long.

It's a framing square. Ever make a figure out of a framing
   square?

Including space and figure together as one entity—that's not
   happening here because you're thinking of it as muscle
   detail.

You've got a nice rolling pattern in here.

If you are *feeling* how that goes together (you may not know
   consciously it's happening) a very beautiful kind of unity will
   happen.

Make a corner. Feel the box in there.

Find the boundaries in the skull where the planes change.

Let's get the head more erect. Trying to be very accurate so we get a sense of what the theme will be. There are several ways to solve it. Just got to try one of them.

Campbell's soup. Standardized. There is that approach. I'd look for doing the drawing from the model. Work on how the eyes perceive. Particularities of that person will lead you to something that's universal.

"It's not my fault, the model moved." Thinking about how many times I've heard that.

McMillan story: *I had a student, and all year I was trying to find the right words to say what he needed to hear. Finally, the last lesson of the year (only 3 students showed up) I found the right words for him and said them. As soon as he heard them, he packed up and left.*

To model: Show us what *you* would like to draw . . . Excellent.

What a beauty, what a beauty, what a beauty.

The abstract shape, 2 or 3 pieces, before you start this stuff.
All the way to the floor.
Fan shape here.

Make the shape, the space included. This is the key. It gives you a rhythm that tells you what's next. Here it tells you: Now, locate the head.

The shapes. Your job is to make them feel—electric.

Push it this way. Longer here. Okay, I'm beginning to get these
   intervals. Get a stick. What does it do—it shows me where
   this bend hits horizontal—then I can see the shape. Makes it
   simpler, so even I can understand.

You're so thick here that you're killing it in here.

You're building all this brickwork, pal, over no foundation.
   You've got to work the legs. I know you don't want to, but
   you've got to.

I like this drawing, it gives me the connector : This diagonal.
   But we have to see this angle correctly. It's simple. Spend
   some time on it anyway. Then you'll know what to do.
   Diagonals are tremendously useful.

You are getting caught up on this piece here. Stepping back will
   help you. If you're going to get stuck on a part, get stuck on
   the largest one.

Wrong shape. You did get the post. Now is the time to make the
   change—otherwise, you're going to have to live with it
   forever. This ought to be the height, this the length. Give me
   some more thickness in herc. Now, this is easier to see than
   yours. Yours has hair and toes and all kinds of distractions
   on it. Mine makes it simpler. You can move your eye around
   on it, it allows clean movements of the eye.

You want to make sure you're okay with it, so put down some
   things that allow you to check it at this stage.

I'm spending a lot of time with that bar there, until it composes.

Details don't make up a drawing. Get some very simple blocks
   together.

You're depending on local arrangements only. Here, why don't you follow this into the movement of this larger element.

Basically, you are seeing the pattern. Keep drawing on that pattern, keep it together, keep using it, see how pieces line up around it, get more mileage out of it. Already your drawing has an austere design impact that should make it easy for you to keep the faith.

Get some value in here. Use the shadow on the wall. You've got a very nice arrangement started, but it doesn't read yet. Keep at it, this is a long term thing.

Which is the biggest section? If we just divide it in half, everything gets too even, and that's not the way it is.

I'm looking for the design of the anatomy, not the anatomy.

Okay, it's got to taper . . . and taller, and taller, and taller.

See this big arc? That's what I'm seeing. I'm responding to that feeling. *McMillan draws arrows along the arc on the student's paper.* 'The Path of the Alewife.' You don't need to figure out an analysis to prove that case.

This is a series of foreshortened forms. Their outlines should show a series of separate, articulated shapes that are somewhat collapsed together.

Foreshortening: What you've got to do to make this drawing work is some very careful measurements. Measurement makes this kind of thing work. Here, if I cut this distance down, I can make the whole head go back. That's a start.

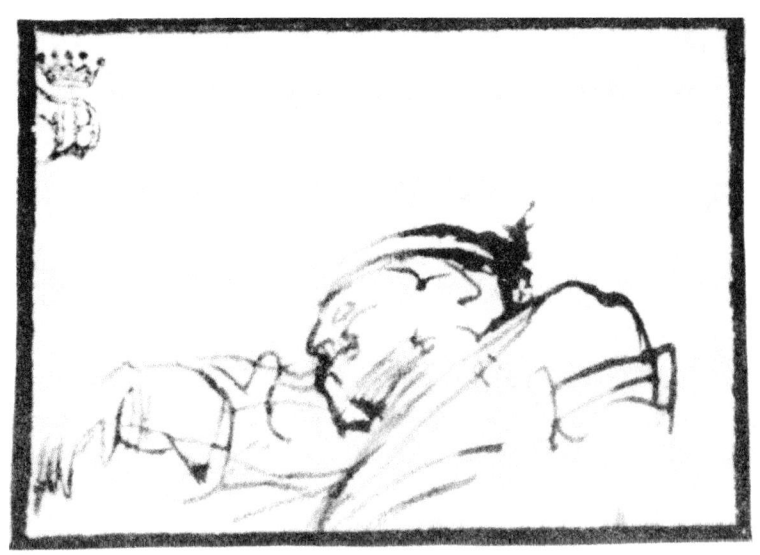

Rembrandt van Rijn

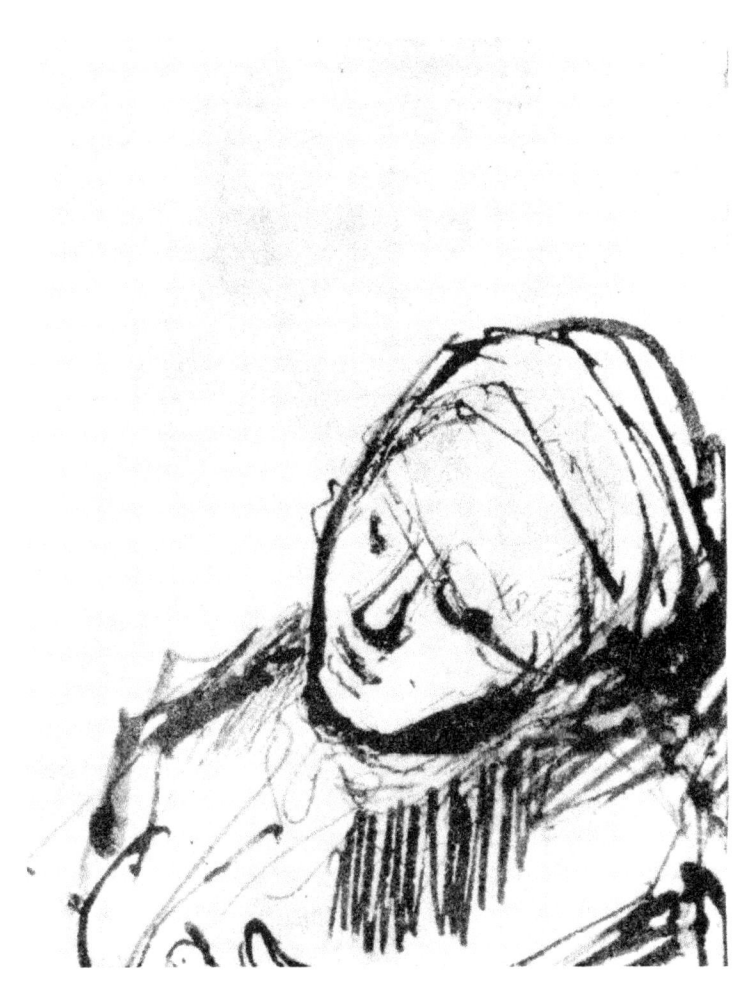

Rembrandt van Rijn

Lesson 13

Push the Drawing Until You Wreck it or You Fix it

First part of session, you want to prepare yourself somehow for drawing. You want to be focused. They used to recommend breathing exercises.

Draw with your whole body, not your wrist.

Look for a structure to hang your drawing on. Then, even if you screw up the drawing, you still have the structure.

I'm so nervous, I've got to put this strong vertical in first thing, right away. It's the corner post of the drawing, the floor will fall in if it's not there.

You've got some gestures, but you have to analyze them and get them in the right place. Make a cage to control them.

You want to bury those parts against each other so you have the tension of them pointing at each other. You're doing a modeling thing in here so I'm losing the tension that comes from the placement.

Go back to your pattern. If you go back to your pattern, you'll be able to put everything in.

Foreshortened figure. Watch out, you'll tend to spread things out vertically.

Convex because flesh presses out. The overall contour of figure is like that. Van Gogh: cusp-like strokes. This is a natural bias: The fullness of form. Living things swell.

Through drawing line: Directional energy, energy from end to end. Make it happen in a connecting line like that.

Watch it there, a little too sharp.
And then, gain your bulk in here—make sense?
See, that holds together as a block.
The clavicle is deeply bowed because he has weight on it.
Feel the light driving. Take your eraser and make that happen.

McMillan to Model: Thank you. These are very open poses, too much so for us now. Take a number that are folded up— closed form.

There's an axis here.

Don't start there, it's too small to help you with the design. See that X? Yeah, go right after that. Square of the shoulders starts another pattern.

Your view: A figure 8, or scissors. Where do they cross.

Doesn't hold together. Don't make: Line here, line there.

Just because you made it doesn't mean you can't eliminate it.

Just get the direction, doesn't have to look like it.

Where the fulcrum of the pair of scissors is, is what you need to establish, rather than all this information it's too early for.

This figure is totally isolated, floating in the center of the sheet. You've got a hell of a lot of paper left over to take care of. When you work on just a small section of the paper, you miss an important design possibility: You don't get to relate the drawing to the sides of the paper . . .

However, in what you have done so far with the figure, you do have a committment to a design, and one advantage of a strong design is that it makes it easier to scale your drawing up. Do that, and it will begin relating to the edges of the sheet.

McMillan to students: Shall we work a little more with the natural light of the skylight? It's going to be dark in this half of the room . . .
Students: Yes.

You've seen it. I suggest you use this piece, which holds from end to end, as the key.

Keep your eye going. See what's hanging on that direction. You started out with that direction, and then you're losing it in here.

Don't talk to yourself 'now I am drawing the back, now I am drawing the leg, now . . .' You'll draw in a jerky way.

You don't have enough of a feeling of the fullness of that Gothic arch there. It keeps arching out, it doesn't really stop.

Look at this as a band. Now we can ask, 'how much of this structure is above it?' See, he begins to sit back. These things are tricky, but you can solve them if you treat objects as horizonatal bands. If you treat them as objects, you can't feel comfortable making the foreshortening.

Vine charcoal: You can push it around easier on the drawing—erases better than compressed charcoal.

With these values, it's a smoky quality you're looking for.

What you want to do is not look at that section, and you'll see its connections. If you insist on looking at it, you lose that ability.

Work the tone a little more until you see the light as an entity. There is a singleness, a unity, to light, as there is to design.

Break that edge in places, bind across it in others.

Draw the stuff that holds it together, not the stuff that tears it apart.

I'm not getting enough of the whole figure leaning. Make estimates and tilt the block he's in. Do the work. It's late in the game, but make it happen.

Things are going to move—don't be afraid to make them move. Push it, push the drawing, until you wreck it or you fix it.

Oh . . . you had a sense of the unity of the light, but now with all this dark heavy modeling you're adding, you're losing that singleness.

Get your full form, strong and connected directions, energy circulating in it.

If you fill yourself up with the unity of the whole and how it flows together, you won't go too far off.

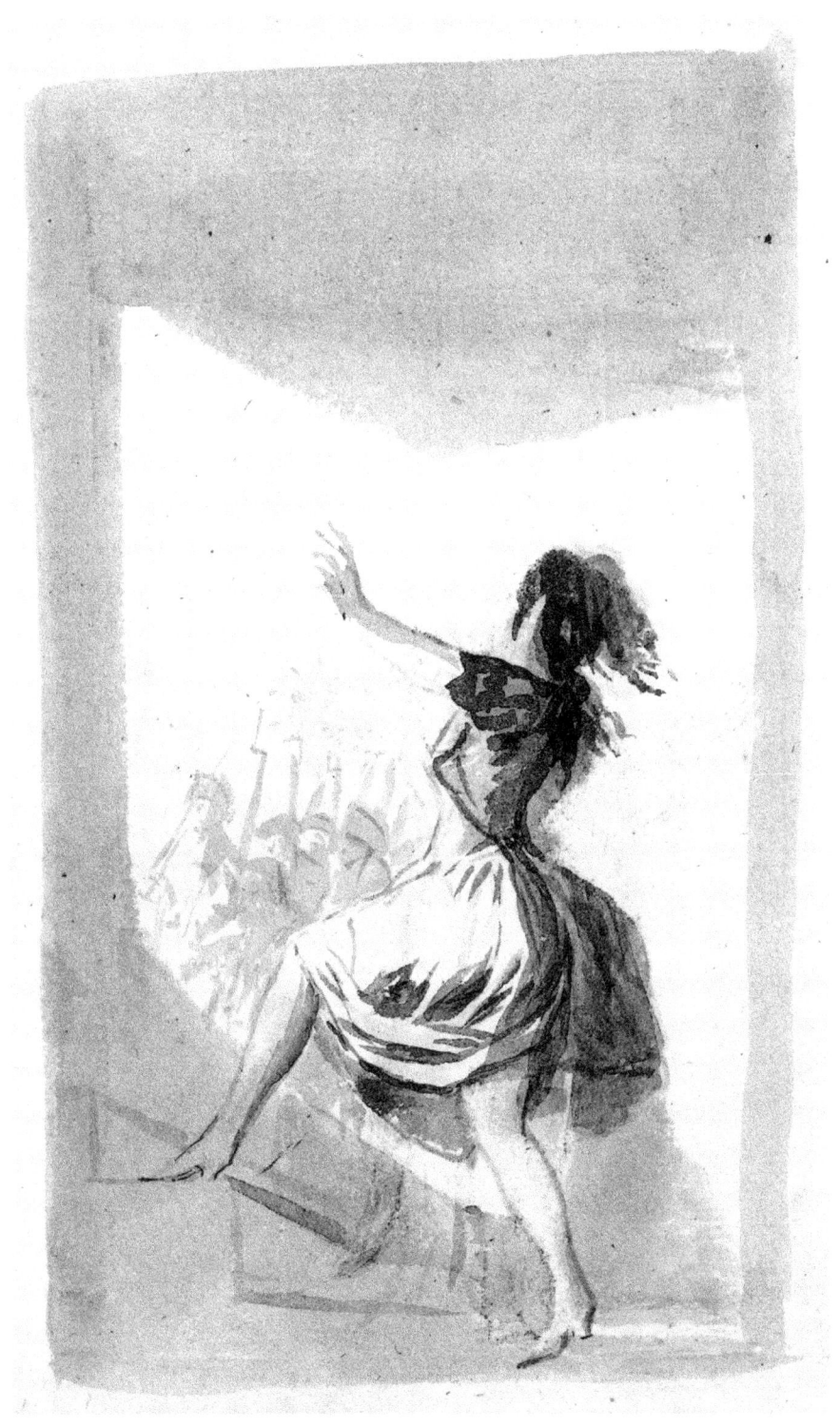

Francisco Jose de Goya y Lucientes

Lesson 14

You've Got to Leave Your Eye Alone to See That

Basically, that's a vertical pose, right?

This is hard. There are a lot of little moves, but you've got to see the big block.

Go right around that form, feel it out and see what it says to you.

What are the important elements. Two or three important elements. See these masses together.

There's a variety of different truths here, therefore try several different approaches.

To the floor. Keep it coming, and get your figure 8. Drop that, push that down. Get enough bulk there that you see it.

But it's also a triangle. Work both together. Squeeze that a little tighter. Build on the comparison.

Don't divide it up so soon. Get this continuous movement first, I mean what's happening from elbow to head.

You're drawing an energy here, as much as anything else. It's a force, an energy you can get out of her pose, that you can get at the truth of in your drawing.

Press this closer together. Shorten this. Then we begin to see these extremities.

Your directions, follow them through so you can get even more information out of them.

More of this, play with this, don't just look at the drawing, be active, nothing is really settled yet.

When you build a set of shapes, there are distortions in them. You just accept them then go around looking for another pattern which will allow you to see a whole other universe, with different distortions, and will help you wiggle out of the former ones.

This is a different plane, and that tone will relate it. Cross the boundary with the tone.

You've got to let your eye alone to see that.

To model: Move your feet. Variety of shapes. Thank you.

Start at the beginning with the blocking. After a session of several drawings, there's a tendency to start as though not at the beginning.

Do two or three large elements, step back and look, step forward and move them around. Back and forth.

The rhythm is bigger.
Make it together, don't make it in little pieces.
Get the shape of the space.
If you see it, put it there. It's the eternal present.
This leg is giving you the strongest direction you have there.
Don't worry about the knees, worry about what puts it together.
This arm is a boundary.
Don't let this have a separate area of its own.
See these masses together, forget that junk.

Take the eraser and draw some light continuity inside the form.
There's a big light plane and a big shadow plane.

Once you look at that pattern for ten minutes, you can't see it
any more. I had you drawing boxes last week. Maybe you
should do that again. Put this away and try a different
approach. You won't lose your identity—but you do want to
be able to crack it a little bit. I mean, that's why you come
here.

That's a different aspect. You used to draw very black. Use both
of them. You can let loose energy, and retain it, both in one
session.

The arm. Oh no, I'm not even looking at the arm, I'm looking at
it as the boundary between what's above it and what's below
it.

You've got to make an adjustment: That band is wider. Don't
wait, don't wait, just do it. Now, once you touch one thing,
you've got to touch a whole series of things. You've got to
work every gear in the alarm clock, or it's not going to ring.

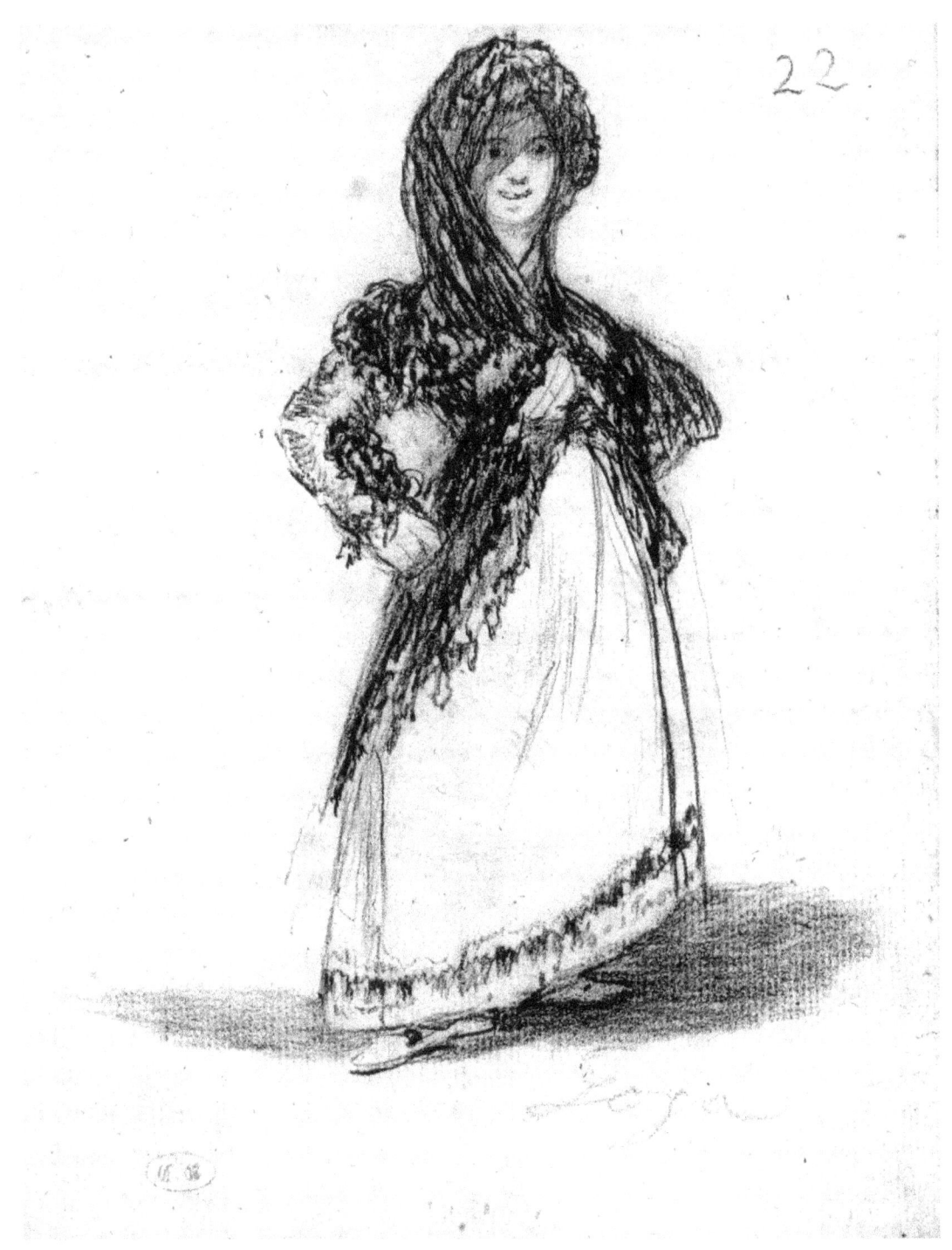

22.

Lesson 15

All That Detail Avalanches Together

The longest thing you can see together, in one stroke.

Make it all at once.

Go to the floor—make him stand. Don't develop the top and just hope the legs will support it.

Don't worry about the features now—there's no way you're going to work on this for a while, with several approaches, and not get the features.

Use the directions off this piece to fit it with with the rest. They give you enough in this case.

Use corners. Back of the skull, use the corner there.

You're too worried about the damn features. You're going to make them, but cumulatively by relations and directions. Get the exact tilt of the head first. That kind of geometry often has more impact than the features, anyway.

You're going to blow some sizes this early in the morning, but if you don't chase them down, it just won't stop.

You have to stay with it—you have to check on it—you can't just put it there and leave it.

As soon as you put that *knee* in there . . . It's that specific look in there that ruins you.

Let it be part of a shape . . . and it goes with this piece.

Go right through, go right across. Nothing is sacrosanct.

You missed the parallelism of this one, which will give you a long box, and you can use that box to tell you more.

Student: Music moves me more than than drawing.
McMillan: Then find the music in the drawing.

To model: Take it down. Size changes. Thank you.

Work it so you don't put it down full blast intensity at first. That's too dark.

Find some pattern you can work it onto. Make a framework. Then you can add that stuff to it.

Okay, are your feet welded there lady? Don't hang over the paper—make sure you do the walking, step back. Now you can see: Move some of these around—a little erasure here, more carbon here. Don't get locked, stay flexible.

Take your time on it—but go from end to end on it even if you are taking your time.

As a unit.

Read the space rather than what's going on with the foreshortened arm etcetera. The space is easier.

As soon as you do that for 30 seconds, spend 30 seconds relating it to the rest of the drawing so that it fits within the compositional elements you've set up. And watch out, you're doing something everybody does: You're enlarging when you focus.

Hmm. You've got these hooked strokes everywhere. Turner does that in his early drawings. He got over it. I mean: Don't impose a response that's solely your own on the work.

Move it, bust it up, don't stay with it.

Push it: 'Okay Joe, a little more over here.'

So I'm looking at this major stuff—all that detail is avalanching in the same direction. It's such a revelation, after years, all that stuff slides together.

When it's so big, you overdo it, and you have to cut it. It's okay.

Put it in there to see it.

You've got to move him. You can't just put it down and have it secure.

You're conscientious enough to worry about the description of the form at this point, but keep the design going. Keep building the whole sweeps, the big organizational facts.

McMillan: You've got to reassert the design over and over. The power is in the design, not in detail. Read the first chapter of Kenneth Clark's <u>The Nude</u>. Staley, what's that Clark phrase?

Staley: "*. . . the sense of simple units, clearly related to one another.*"

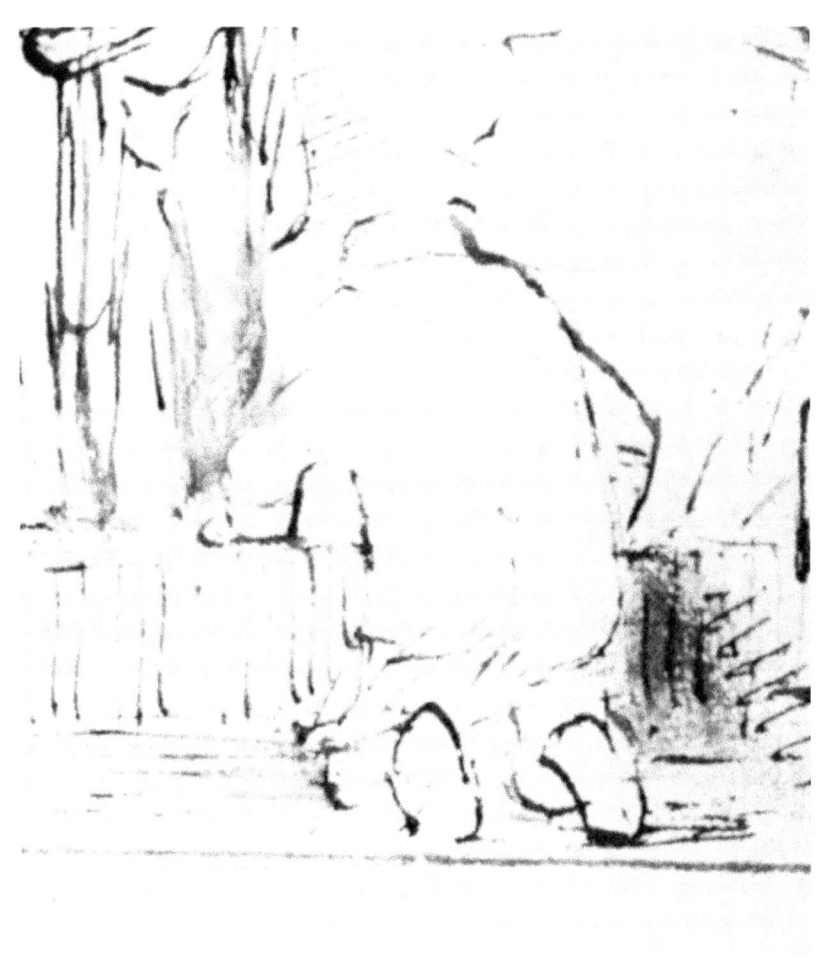

Lesson 16

Intoxicate Yourself with the Feeling of the Piece

Get the entire length, find something that will give you the entire length, even if you have to invent something.

Stay with the big thing until you get the arrangement.

It's a little wrist move. That is not going to let you feel this piece. The only one that is, is from the shoulder or deeper.

This line doesn't give you the feeling of the piece, whereas these do give you the feeling of the piece. You want to empathetically identify with the piece.

Too complicated, right away. Get the big rhythm first, so it holds together.

I'm lengthening this motive to compare it to that motive. I'm setting it up so I can make judgments.

Don't just draw the right side, tie it to the left side at the same time. That one you've taken to the ground, why don't you take this one to the ground too, then you'll get the thickness of the rib cage.

The vase aspect of this thing: This against this.

Intoxicate yourself with those shapes from the beginning, then you won't desert them.

It comes forth in how you feel about it. Key your own feeling in your body to what's going on here.

Too small to use. Find your weight-carrying structure first. Use the weight-holding leg and drive it through where it goes, drive it right on through.

You're looking at it sequentially, through a microscope, one piece at a time. You need to look at it in a unified kind of way. You can learn, we can teach you, but you've got to have faith.

It's piecemeal.
Treat this as a unit. You're trying to render it too soon.
Pull this together, tie it together.
Not so much of a corner here. More of a corner here.
This one is different—you've got a shape with an axis on it.
Set this configuration in here, then slope it as a whole.
Much harder to make vertical judgments than horizontal ones.

Stay with the larger pieces—your pieces are too small.
Student: Like, 2 or 3, or, 4 pieces?
McMillan: yes.

Okay—but get a head on her that's hers. Locate it. Don't slap on some paper bag.

Don't draw the foot at this stage, draw the position of it, then its relation to other shapes, and then, if you must, put a toe on it.

You're just pushing the outline. You want a classy silhouette, but you're just flattening the drawing. Get some other activities, and try to move around in your drawing instead of tracing.

Don't give me information about that rib cage yet because it's going to interfere with relating it. Haul it together as a block.

You're tickling it. Rather than tickle it, start another drawing.

If you see it, put it there, even if you don't know what it is.

You're still thinking of the head as an addition, and it doesn't work. Locate it.

You're making lines, you're depicting parts. You have to go back to your blocks. The blocking should be there in the end, because it's your structure.

Now how does that feel! You're no longer thinking of the head as an addition. You've got a Cathedral there instead of something decapitated.

See, you want to develop that rib cage, and you're doing it at the expense of the rest of your drawing.

McMillan: Watch just drawing darker and darker lines.
Student: But that's how I push things around.
McMillan: Okay. Then start out lighter.

This does as you suggest. Go around the whole shape. Have to see these together.

Go around the rotary three times and figure which way to get out: Give it the time.

Don't do something that perpetrates a wrong against that gestural rhythm you're starting to get down. You want to grasp an overall gestural feeling: When you get it, it will echo through the whole the drawing.

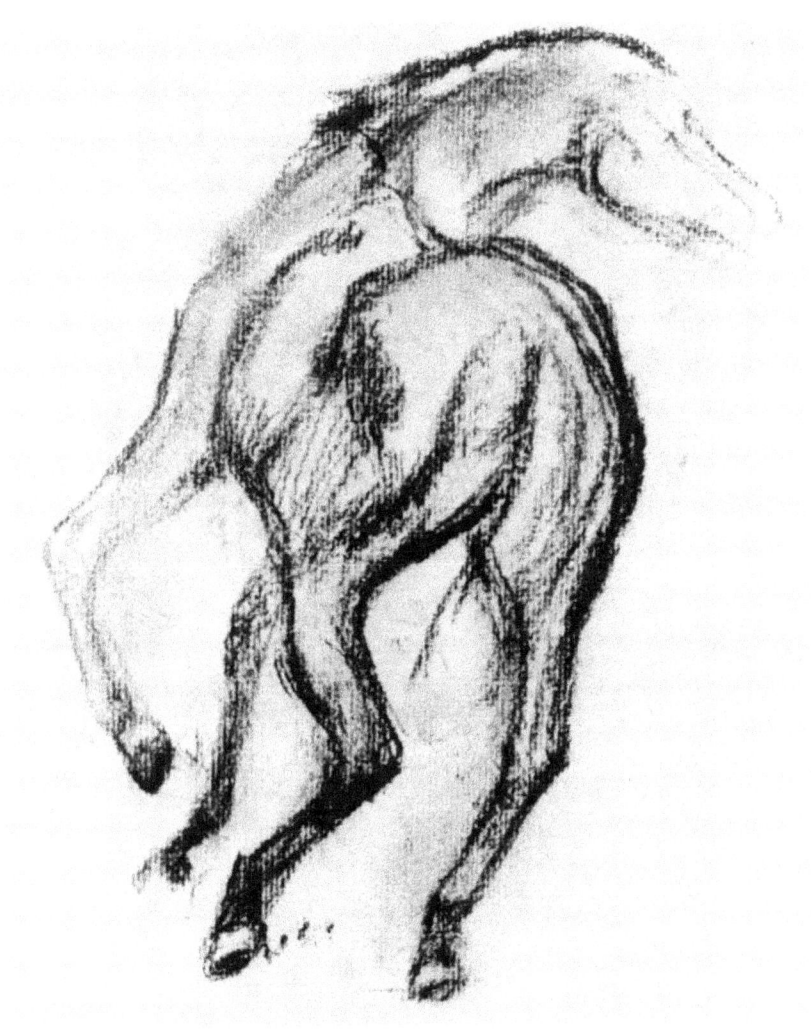

Edgar Degas

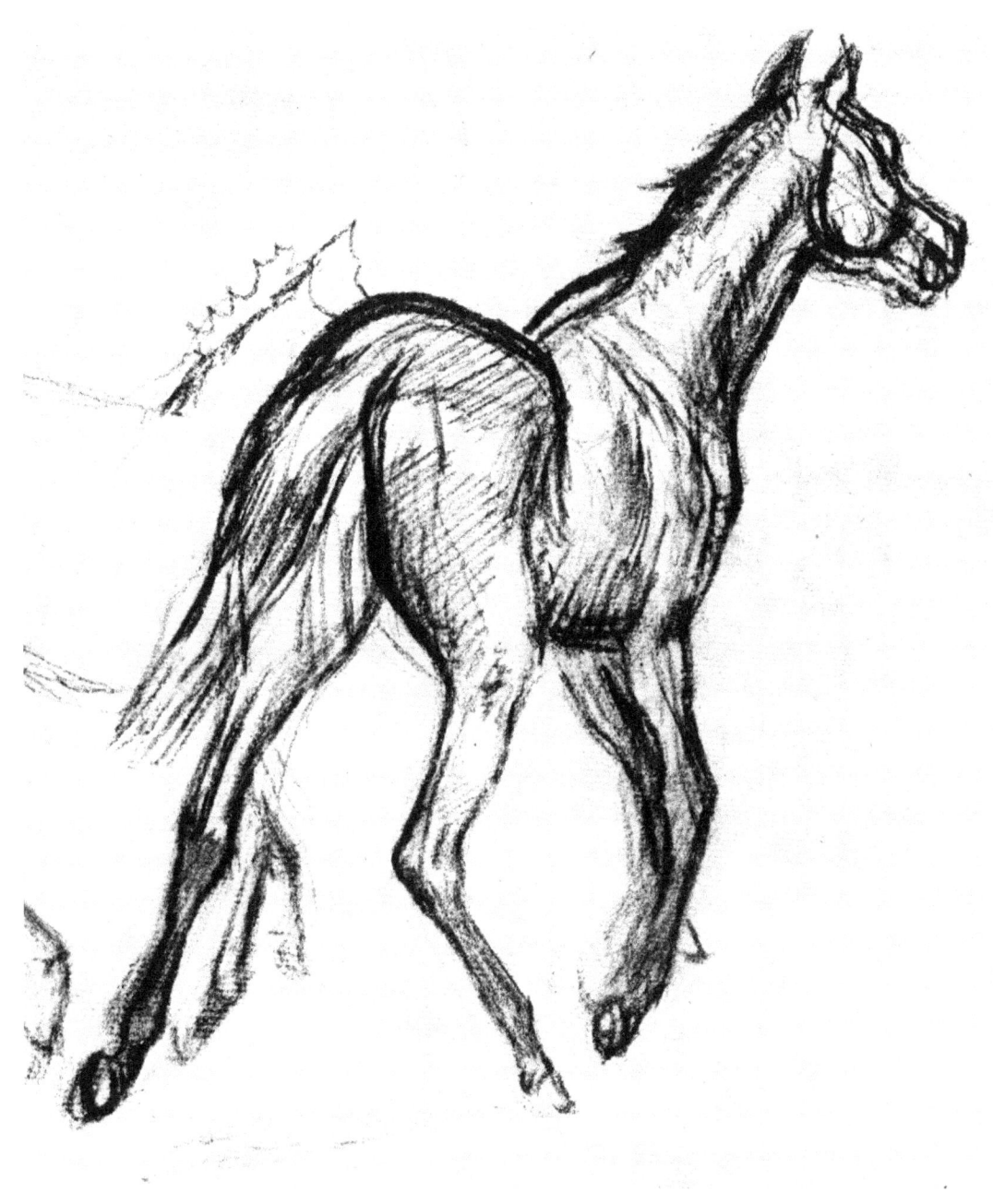

Edgar Degas

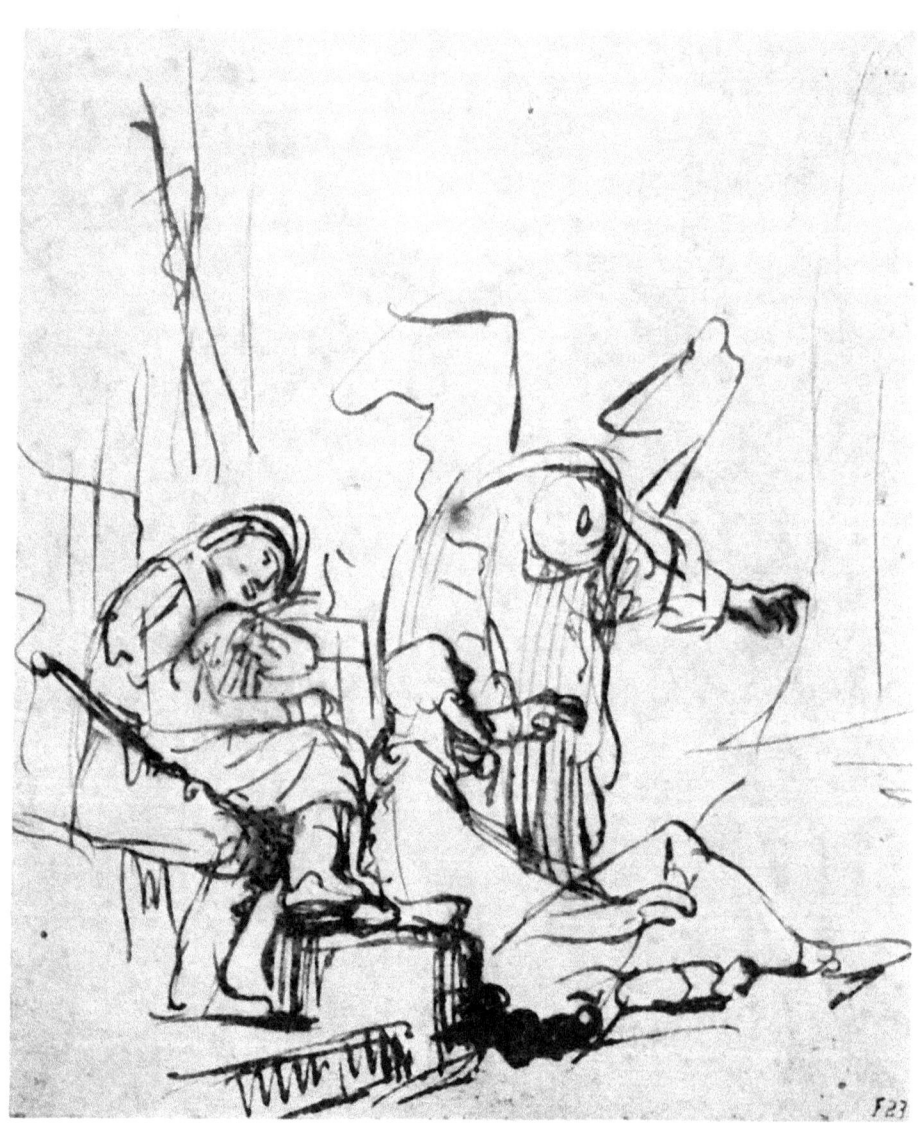

110   Rembrandt van Rijn

Lesson 17

Not, This *Then* That. This *And* That.

Get yourself warmed up. Don't let me harass you too much.

The whole figure at once. You say to yourself, 'I can't do that.' But you can. How? *Just do it.*

Very circular pattern up here. You don't see it, and it'll break into segments. Include the head with it.

Yes, okay, but even more together. Not, this *then* that. This *and* that. Not, *this* and 10,000 years later, *that*.

The circle you get in the shoulders is going to continue down there, in the legs. Even more fluent. Enhance that curve. Don't be afraid to let it go over here, how else are you going to find out? You don't just decide, you don't know until you try it.

Not just a curve any curve, but a curve that has this aspect to it, that it makes you look across the whole unity of the piece. And in fact the process of making the piece is the process of the discovery of such hidden structural elements and hidden emotional elements.

You want to get a sense of what those big angles are.

She leans. How come you haven't got a lean? It should be the first thing you do. You miss that by seeing too particularly at the beginning. In the beginning, you only know a few important things.

It's tipped. This way. You have it the opposite.

Leaning wagon wheel about to come off.

You're looking at this alone. Don't make this thing all by itself.

Okay. Don't grasp at it too hard, too fast.

See this S? Take it through the center. Now, what's so astounding about it is the head swings the other way. Is that enough for you? You need that motive.

Just that move does quite a lot for you. I'm looking at it in relation to the whole piece now. You've got to look at different scales moment by moment and fit them inside each other. I know I say not to look at detail, but of course you have to—but not for long, not for 15 minutes.

To model: Make a shape. Thank you.

Ah, this pose. See, if the ends crossed on a raindrop, that's what it would look like.

All the way out to the end, where it's going. Okay, don't stay out there and contemplate it, get out of there and make shapes. What other direction relates to that extremity?

Elevate the bottom of the rib cage above the pelvic crest more than you have, at least two or three inches more. A wide separation there distinguishes us from the apes. It's a very beautiful area of the human body, and it makes us wonderfully flexible at the waist, makes us dancers, lookouts, while the apes are stiff there, can't twist or lean or stretch at the waist much at all.

Don't think. Don't put all those words in there. You've got to get *this* direction, *now*. Take it right off the model, hold your stick up.

You're trying to finish it before you get it laid out. Spend more time laying it out. If you get it laid out right, you'll need very little time to finish it.

Now, when you alter something like this, you have to do the whole drawing again, because relations depended on that. Do we still have the arms on? Probably not. So we have to go back and struggle.

Get it so you can see how they relate, those big block sizes.
What you're doing with this bow shape isn't emphatic enough.
Okay, if your sizes were better.
This isn't settled yet.
Get the sense of these being near parallels.
Planes have priority. Later, you can render around them.

Nothing is right till you're done with it, when they all fit together at the end.

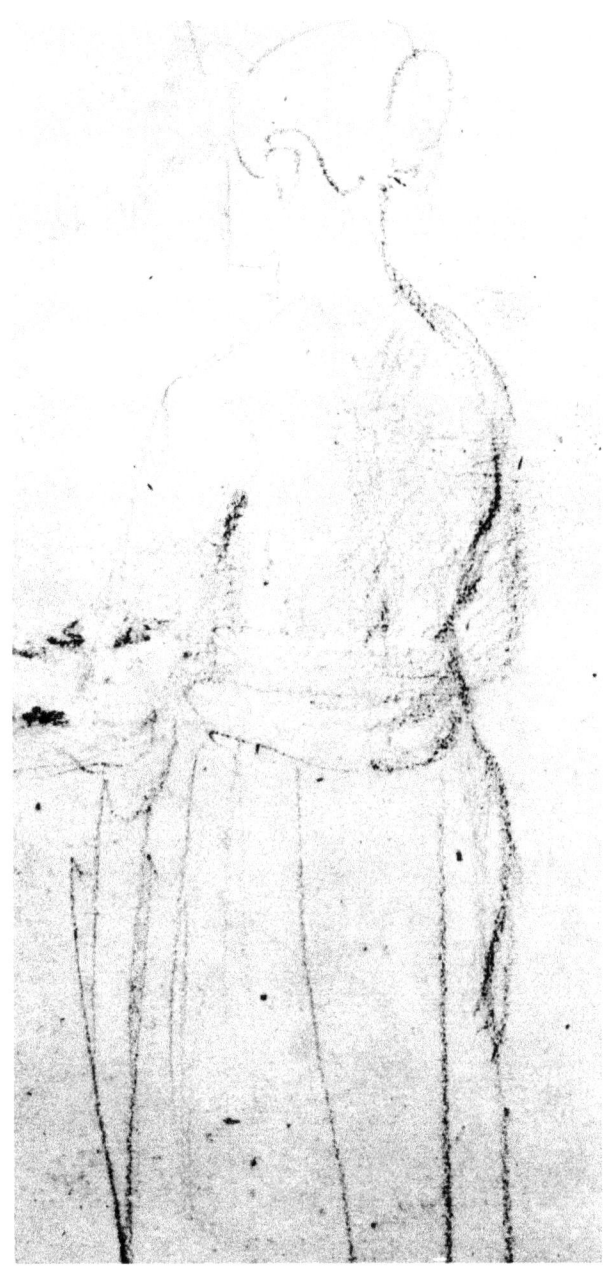

Rembrandt van Rijn

Lesson 18

Put it Down and Take a Beating

Set your drawing up, don't just begin to draw.

Make it stand first, before you go in there and draw.

If you draw from your wrist, you're dead. Your body's not involved, and you can't stand back.

Don't get too complicated. Take this and drive it right to the heel.

Keep on working on it until you make it stand.

Figure 8 business. Keep these movements together.

No, no, no. You're coloring the thighs. No coloring and no rendering at this stage.

See what I'm doing? I've got the movements now, but not the sizes.

You can reduce it to an abstraction, you don't have to do only the illusionistic. You can do both.

Get that pattern, get that design. A full sheet . . . to the floor.

You're thinking: "Two arms," rather than, "One shape."

Do not go in there and render and color this stuff. It's a construction first. I'm training you in *making things go together*. The whole surface must hold together as plastic form, not just description. All the whole pieces fit together, and this is not to be buried by coloring. Watch out, black and white unity, unity of value, can camouflage whatever errors of structure there are. You want your drawing to look just as bad as it can so you can see what's wrong with it, instead of covering it up with coloring.

You need this corner, it's like air, you can't do without it.

And here, you're having this problem because you're looking at it with your mind's eye, frontally . . . like an Egyptian.

Hallway discussion during break. Staley shows McMillan a print he made from a drawing:

McMillan: You learn your drawing, you take it to heart. Don't use it once and turn it under, see what else it will give you. Find ways of simplifying it, find a core pattern. Reverse figure and ground. Change the angles, the sizes. Theme and variations. Send it again and again through the processes, long row of trials, work like washing dishes. Don't stop when you find one you like. Alfred Barr on Matisse working, 20 photos. Let it keep taking you further. Make it give you stuff you didn't know it could.

Staley: Thank you. . . . I'll never make prints that way.

McMillan: You might. You don't know.

To model: Closed form. Thank you.

You've got to feel it from the first instant.
How wide for how tall.
You're looking too soon at this. Draw it with something else.
You need to go to the ends.
Drive your directions through.
Get this part, this is your biggest part.
You're seeing too much in there.
Don't separate this.
You're looking at them as bits and pieces too much.
This you looked at too hard. Take it with the thing it goes with.

Good, Tom. You're willing to put it down and take a beating, more than you have been for some time.

Don't only work the top piece, make them together. When the top and bottom don't fit, go back and forth between them. I don't know any other way to do it.

Hmm. You can solve that detail, but you can't solve the drawing by it.

You're hitting it harder and harder on the edges, making it flatter and flatter. You want to bust these edges open and make things happen *inside* the form. Push, then let up where the flesh turns, push again, series of interrupted stuff, not a complete outline that surrounds, cripples, isolates.

You're seeing too much, in too fine a way, then not seeing the big design. Take three steps back. Remember: Rhythm of work, then three steps back.

You're wanting to *finish* it because you're a painter, and that's a painter's practice. Paintings often cover over the interesting things.

You've got to look at the blocking all the way through.

This is the end, the stage at which everything shows up, everything you've glossed over.

Rembrandt, Goya, Degas at the end of life: Flexible invention of style. Improvisation. Versus stiff, locked in. At the end, Degas would crumple a piece of paper and drop it on the floor and draw it: Came out as a human figure.

Rembrandt and Goya, at the end: Singing through their body and their blood.

You never stop learning to draw.

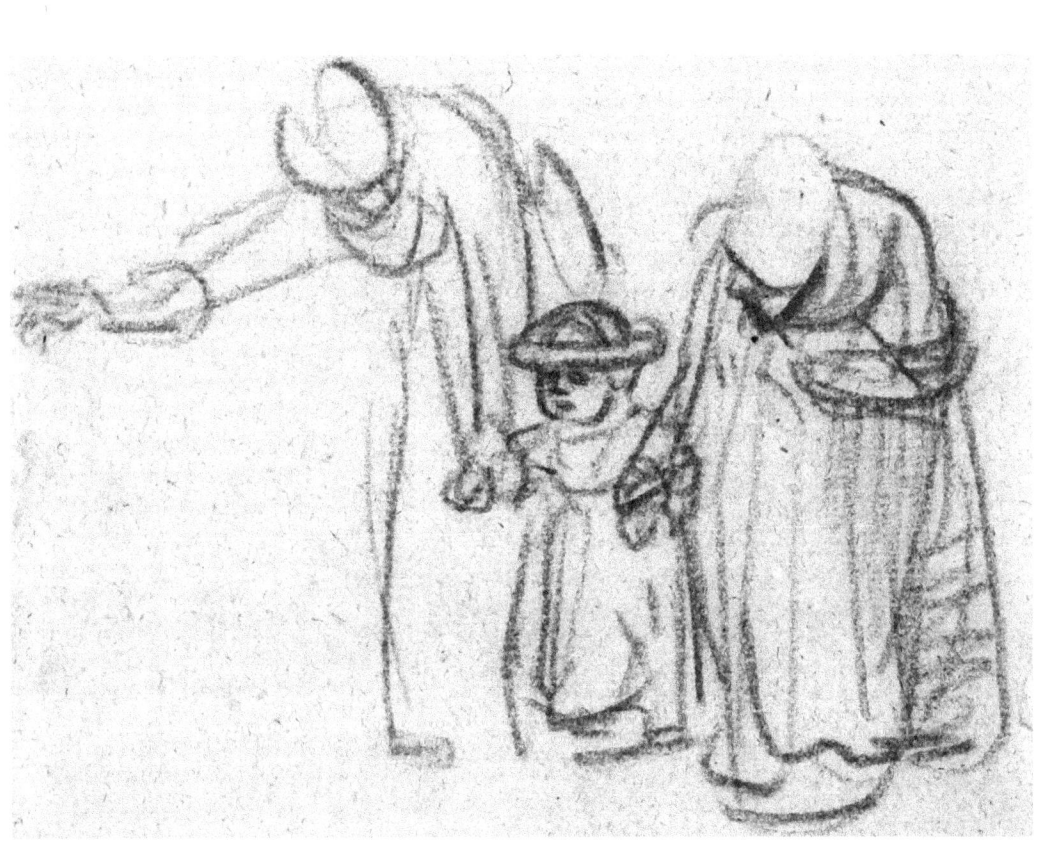

Rembrandt van Rijn   121

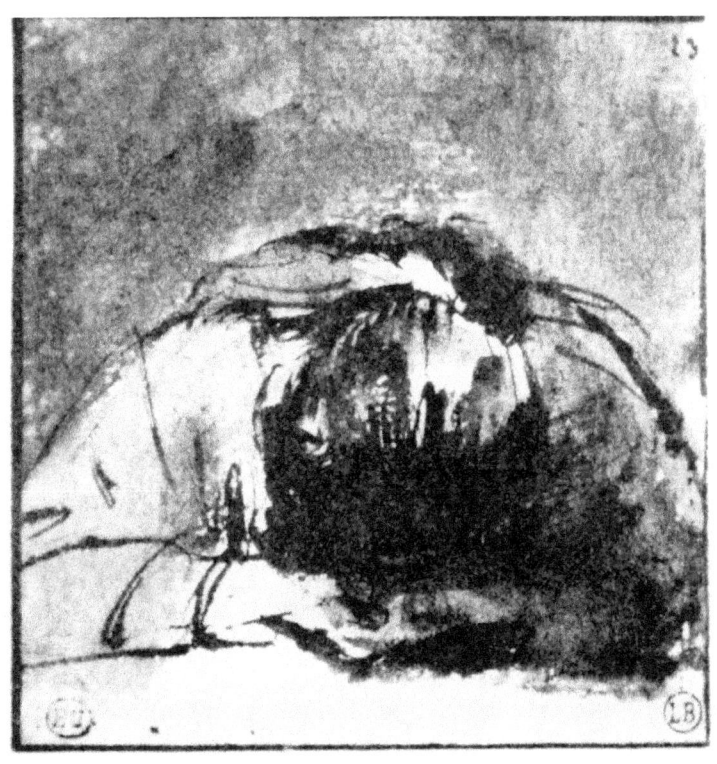

Rembrandt van Rijn   123

List of Drawings

Some of the drawings have been cropped and/or enlarged.

Front Cover: Rembrandt van Rijn (1606-1669)
Red chalk, grey wash
Benesch Cat. No. 448
Berlin, Kupferstichkabinett

Back Cover: Rembrandt van Rijn
Pen and bistre
Benesch Cat. No. 35
London, British Museum

p. 11   Rembrandt van Rijn
Pen and bistre
Benesch Cat. No. 938
Collection: Comtes Palatins du Rhin

p. 17   Rembrandt van Rijn
Pen and bistre
Benesch Cat. No. 70
London, British Museum

p. 23   Rembrandt van Rijn
Pen and brush in bistre
Benesch Cat. No. 1107
Munich, Graphische Sammlung

p. 24   Rembrandt van Rijn
Red chalk
Benesch Cat. No. 152
Amsterdam, Rijksprentenkabinet

p. 29   Edgar Degas (1834-1917)   Study for portrait of Martelli
Pencil
Biblioteque National, Paris

In Memoriam Andrew T. McMillan, Andy, 1936-2009

Teacher, Mentor, Friend

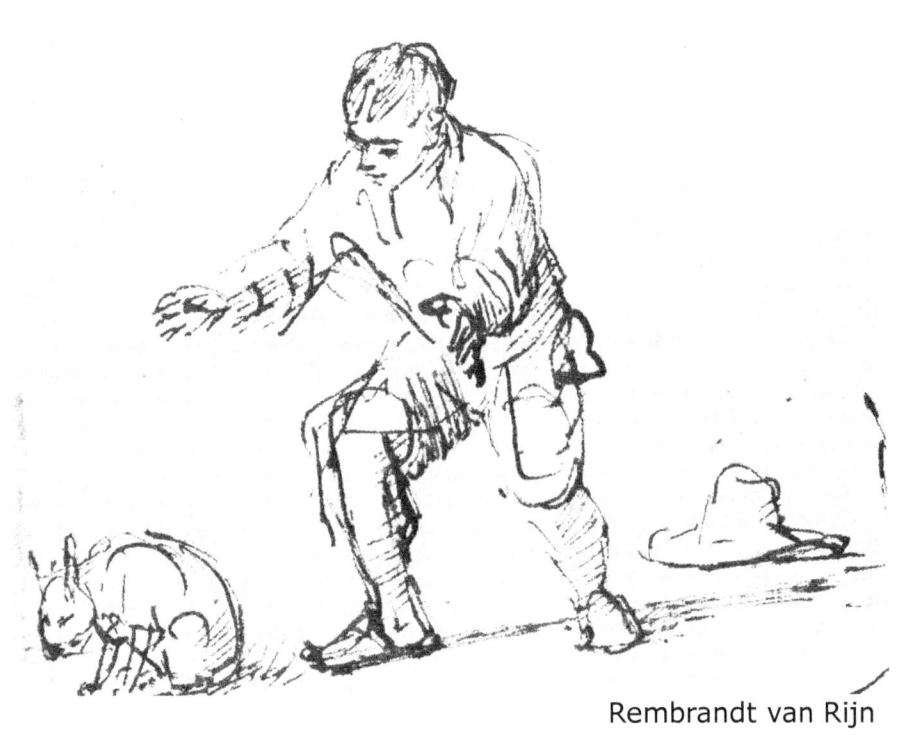

Rembrandt van Rijn